The Battle of Ole Miss

....

The Battle of Ole Miss

....

Civil Rights v. States' Rights

FRANK LAMBERT

Purdue University

New York   Oxford

OXFORD UNIVERSITY PRESS

2010

Oxford University Press, Inc., publishes works that further Oxford University's
objective of excellence in research, scholarship, and education.

Oxford   New York
Auckland   Cape Town   Dar es Salaam   Hong Kong   Karachi
Kuala Lumpur   Madrid   Melbourne   Mexico City   Nairobi
New Delhi   Shanghai   Taipei   Toronto

With offices in
Argentina   Austria   Brazil   Chile   Czech Republic   France   Greece
Guatemala   Hungary   Italy   Japan   Poland   Portugal   Singapore
South Korea   Switzerland   Thailand   Turkey   Ukraine   Vietnam

Published by Oxford University Press, Inc.
198 Madison Avenue, New York, New York 10016
http://www.oup.com

Oxford is a registered trademark of Oxford University Press

Library of Congress Cataloging-in-Publication Data

Lambert, Frank, 1943–
    The battle of Ole Miss : civil rights v. states' rights / Frank Lambert.
        p.   cm.—(Critical historical encounters)
    ISBN 978–0–19–538041–5—ISBN 978–0–19–538042–2
1. University of Mississippi—History.   2. Meredith, James, 1933–
3. College integration—Mississippi—Oxford—History.
4. African Americans—Civil rights—Mississippi—Oxford—History.
5. Civil rights—Mississippi—Oxford—History.   I. Title.
    LD3413.L36 2009
    378.762'83—dc22   2009004339

Printing number: 9 8 7 6 5 4 3 2 1

Printed in the United States of America
on acid-free paper

For Beth

CONTENTS

....

EDITOR'S FOREWORD

....

The volumes in this Oxford University Press book series focus on major critical encounters in the American experience. The word "critical" refers to formative, vital, transforming events and actions that have had a major impact in shaping the ever-changing contours of life in the United States. "Encounter" indicates a confrontation or clash, oftentimes but not always contentious in character, but always full of profound historical meaning and consequence.

In this framework, the United States, it can be said, has evolved on contested ground. Conflict and debate, the clash of peoples and ideas, have marked and shaped American history. The first Europeans transported with them cultural assumptions that collided with Native American values and ideas. Africans forced into bondage and carried to America added another set of cultural beliefs that often were at odds with those of Native Americans and Europeans. Over the centuries America's diverse peoples differed on many issues, often resulting in formative conflict that in turn gave form and meaning to the American experience.

The Critical Historical Encounters series emphasizes formative episodes in America's contested history. Each volume contains two fundamental ingredients: a carefully written narrative of the encounter and the consequences, both immediate and long-term, of that moment of conflict in America's contested history.

In *The Battle of Ole Miss: Civil Rights v. States' Rights*, Frank Lambert returns to one of the Civil Rights' battlefields. In the fall semester of 1962, James Meredith, a determined African American who wanted to graduate from his state's university, sought to enroll in the lily-white University of Mississippi. Opposed to Meredith was the state's governor Ross Barnett, members of the White Citizens Council and the Ku Klux Klan, and, it sometimes seemed, virtually the entire white population of the state of Mississippi. Although the administration of President John F. Kennedy supported Meredith's admission, the federal presence in Oxford was certainly insufficient to either fully protect Meredith or prevent violent demonstrations. Meredith's act was one of courage, an insistence that America should fulfill its loftiest ideals.

Frank Lambert is a historian today, but in 1962 he was a student at the University of Mississippi. As a person who was born and raised in segregated Mississippi and witnessed "the battle of Ole Miss" he is perfectly positioned to write about the reality and the meaning of the event. He felt the heat of the fires set on campus, saw the rage in the faces of the protestors, and has had decades to reflect upon what it all meant. As a result, his narrative of the events contains both an eyewitness account and an historian's perspective.

ACKNOWLEDGMENTS

....

This book has been a collaborative effort from conception to publication, and I have many individuals to thank for their contributions along the way. My colleague and co-editor of this series, Randy Roberts, encouraged me to write the book in the first place. I am grateful to him for what has been a most satisfying professional undertaking as well as a profoundly personal experience. I was a student at Ole Miss when the principal events of this book took place, and revisiting them as a professional historian has been both rewarding and challenging. I am also indebted to Oxford University Press Acquisitions Editor Brian Wheel for guiding the project through the publication process from proposal submission through final production, offering invaluable suggestions about organization and writing along the way.

I owe a debt of gratitude to the numerous archivists and librarians who helped me immeasurably in finding and using research materials. I am especially indebted to those men and women working in the Archives and Special Collections at a number of Mississippi institutions, including the University of Mississippi, Mississippi State University, the University of Southern Mississippi, and Alcorn State University. All of them displayed the highest professional competency and extended their expertise with gracious helpfulness.

The highlight of my research was meeting and interviewing James Meredith. I found him to be open, charming, and forthright in discussing the events of 1962. He provided invaluable insight into his motivation, strategy, hopes, and fears in challenging segregation at Ole Miss.

My greatest debt is to my wife Beth, who as always provided steadfast support. She accompanied me on trips to Mississippi, provided helpful suggestions about research strategy, and offered constructive criticism of the text. On a more personal level, she, as always, offered much needed perspective and encouragement.

The Battle of Ole Miss

....

INTRODUCTION

While working in the Civil Rights and Race Relations Collection located on the third floor of the University of Mississippi Library early in 2008, I happened to look out the window onto a scene unimaginable 45 years earlier when the events that inspired this book transpired. An African American student was conducting a campus tour for a small group of prospective students and their parents, all of whom were white. I watched the group listening attentively to the guide, asking questions, and following his gestures as he pointed to various buildings. Then he opened the doors to the white-columned Lyceum Building, which houses the university's administrative offices, and ushered his guests inside. What made the scene not only noteworthy, but poignant for me was the memory of what had happened at that very spot when I was a second-year undergraduate at Ole Miss. The Lyceum was ground zero in a bloody battle that took place on the night of September 30, 1962, between perhaps a couple thousand staunch segregationists, mainly nonstudents, and federal marshals and federalized Mississippi National Guardsmen, who were on campus to ensure the safety of James Meredith, a black Mississippian who was seeking admission.

The noted Yale historian Edmund Morgan once stated that people searching the past often find what they are looking for. That is, our interests, shaped by our cultural values, aspirations, beliefs, and prejudices, shape our fields of vision. As a student and member of the Ole Miss football team in 1962, I was far more interested in the fortunes of our team than in James Meredith's quest to become the first African American student. Thus, I was one of the self-absorbed students who remained passive as extremists set the course of events. Now, almost 50 years after the events of fall 1962, I recognize the historic significance of what James Meredith did as well as the incredible courage that he exhibited. So I returned to Ole Miss to conduct research for a book that I hope will provide a guided tour of that critical historical encounter between a lone black person's fight for equal opportunity and the violent resistance he met from whites determined to maintain white supremacy and racial segregation in all the state's schools.

James Meredith applied for admission in 1961, but university officials first set aside, then challenged, and finally denied his application. When he persisted in his quest, state officials, including Governor Ross Barnett, became involved and launched an all-out legal battle to ensure that the state's flagship university remained segregated. But James Meredith was as determined in pursuit of his civil rights as Ross Barnett was in defending states' rights. The 29-year-old Air Force veteran, who was transferring from all-black Jackson State University, pinned his hopes on John F. Kennedy's willingness to send troops to Ole Miss, if necessary, much as President Eisenhower had done in Little Rock in 1957 to protect nine African Americans who wished to attend Central High School there. Though reluctant to take on the myriad calls from across the South for federal assistance in support of civil rights for African Americans, especially those calling for desegregation of schools, Kennedy, at the urging of the NAACP's Thurgood Marshall, reluctantly agreed to Meredith's plea.

For more than a year and a half, Meredith's case dragged on in the federal court system. Finally, in September 1962 a federal judge ordered Governor Barnett and university officials to admit him forthwith. His admission, however, was anything but peaceful; indeed, he entered Ole Miss only after a bloody battle. The hours and days surrounding that battle on September 30, 1962, are confusing and difficult to fathom. Certainly for many outsiders—that is, those living outside Mississippi—events that night at Ole Miss underscored their view that Mississippi was a land apart from the rest of the United

Governor Ross Barnett defending states' rights; James Meredith seeking civil rights.
© Bettmann/Corbis

States. And Mississippians' perceptions of those same events were distorted as well, blurred by a cultural myopia developed over more than a hundred years.

This book is an attempt to understand the events at Ole Miss in 1962 by examining them primarily from the perspective of students. It is a story largely about students written primarily for students. It is about one black student's overcoming daunting opposition to become the first of his race to matriculate at the university. It is also about thousands of white students who resisted James Meredith's joining the student body. It seeks to understand why Meredith deemed it important enough to risk his life to enter a school where he was not wanted. And, it seeks to understand why white students feared integration, especially in 1962, almost a decade after *Brown v. Board of Education*, at a time when most southern states had desegregated their schools or, more accurately, had reluctantly instituted token desegregation in the face of continuing intractability by whites. To find answers, the book traces the separate social and cultural paths that Meredith and the white students traveled that ended in their confrontation at Ole Miss. But the book is more than a story of students; it is a chapter in two big struggles that provide the context for the events of 1962: Mississippi's states' rights claims, with roots extending back to the Civil War and Reconstruction, and African Americans' struggle for full civil rights, also grounded in Reconstruction. The desegregation of Ole Miss, then, is a case study that examines the struggle for and resistance to civil rights in the most intractable state. By looking closely at the battle of Ole Miss, a single incident, the book examines a moment that illuminates broader themes: social and cultural fault lines fundamental to understanding American federalism, Mississippi race relations, the fight for racial justice, and the political realignment that transformed the South from "yellow dog Democrats" to Nixon Republicans. It is a multilayered narrative about an individual's struggle, a university's survival, a state's continuation of a century-old war, and a federal administration's reluctant but resolute protection of one man's civil rights.

James Meredith had dreamed of going to Ole Miss since he was a 14-year-old boy growing up on a farm outside Kosciusko, named fittingly for an earlier freedom fighter, General Thaddeus Kosciusko, a Polish military engineer who fought in America's War of Independence. Like many other teenagers, he had big plans—first to become a lawyer and then to be elected governor—and an Ole Miss degree was an important first step in fulfilling those ambitions. The overwhelming majority of lawyers and politicians in the state were graduates of the state's oldest and most prestigious university. Meredith's application for admission in December 1961 was straightforward for an in-state transfer student; he had amassed enough credits during his years in the Air Force to enter as a junior, and his academic record clearly met the university's standards. Moreover, his family was respectable and his parents were law-abiding citizens whose taxes helped support the university. Yet Meredith knew for a fact that his application would be denied. He was an African American, and the university had never admitted a black student in its more than 100-year existence.

Meredith was not the first black person to apply to one of Mississippi's white universities, and he was fully aware of how the handful of others had been treated. University and state officials had cajoled, bribed, and intimidated his predecessors into withdrawing their applications. One who persisted despite the pressure found himself committed to the state mental hospital at Whitfield, and another landed in the state penitentiary at Parchman on trumped-up criminal charges. White Mississippians had a long history of "taking care" of "uppity" blacks who attempted to transgress sacred racial boundaries. After the collapse of Reconstruction in the 1870s, the state in 1890 drafted a constitution that called for strict segregation of the races, including separate schools for whites and blacks. Armed with that constitutional authority and imbued with the firm conviction of white supremacy, state officials used every means within their power, plus some that were outside the law, to enforce segregation. One brutal but effective means employed to intimidate blacks and keep them in their place was lynching. The greatest incidence of lynchings in the state occurred during the period 1890 to 1910, with a peak of 25 lynchings in 1904. In the years 1904 to 1908, there was an average of one lynching every 25 days. The terror succeeded. Many blacks left the state, and those who stayed were careful to stay well within the prescribed race boundaries. Such terror, coupled with the lack of economic opportunity, spurred mass emigration; almost one million blacks left Mississippi between 1910 and 1960, hoping for a better life in such booming northern industrial cities as Detroit and Chicago. Those who stayed behind learned how to survive within Mississippi's harsh racial code.[1]

It is within that history of violence and exodus that James Meredith confronted Mississippi's entrenched segregation. He defied the state's harsh racial code by refusing to accept the rejection from Ole

Miss that in fact arrived in his mail, and that is why his story is so captivating and central to the fight for civil rights in Mississippi. By filing suit in federal courts and doggedly pursuing his admission for more than a year and a half, he confronted the most southern state in the nation, and arguably the most racist. He pursued his quest for full civil rights with the same determination that Governor Ross Barnett defended segregation in the name of states' rights. The historic confrontation between Meredith and Barnett is the subject of this book and serves as a framework for answering some larger questions facing Mississippians and indeed all Americans in the early 1960s. Why would Meredith risk his life by attempting to transfer from all-black Jackson State College to the University of Mississippi? What did he hope to gain, and would the cost be worth it? Why did hundreds of white students at Ole Miss hurl the vilest racial insults at Meredith as well as throw bricks at federal marshals who tried to ensure his safety? Why would Governor Barnett appeal to the most extreme elements in the state, including the Citizens' Councils and the Ku Klux Klan, in his campaign to keep Ole Miss all-white? Why did the majority of white Mississippians, decent and law-abiding, acquiesce in the governor's race-baiting and unlawful behavior by remaining silent and passive? Why did the federal government spend millions of dollars and dispatch more than 10,000 troops to the Ole Miss campus to ensure Meredith's safety? And, what difference did this one historic confrontation make in the bigger history of race relations, federalism, and the fight for civil rights?

The search for answers involves interwoven stories. At one level, it is the story of an historic encounter between two individuals: James Meredith and Governor Ross Barnett. Each stood up for what he thought was right—Meredith for civil rights guaranteed by the United States Constitution and Barnett for states' rights as set forth in the Mississippi Constitution. It is the story of a courageous individual who staked all in quest of a dream and a tenacious leader who strove to maintain racial segregation while at the same time keeping extremists from resorting to violence. At many moments, James Meredith wondered if he could persevere in the face of unrelenting opposition and virulent hatred, while Ross Barnett worried that his power was slipping away to the federal government and to radical elements in Mississippi.

But this is more than the story of two individuals. Standing behind each of the protagonists were large numbers of people who pinned their hopes on the outcome of the struggle represented by Meredith and Barnett. Behind Meredith were generations of African Americans who had longed for the day that their children would have the same opportunities for a good education and a good job that white parents had wanted for their offspring. Also behind him were the hundreds of activists in Mississippi's civil rights movement, a movement that made martyrs of many in Meredith's lifetime. Meredith also stood for the hundreds of black students who, while he fought for admission to Ole Miss, risked all to desegregate public facilities, end employment discrimination, and register blacks to vote. Behind Barnett was the majority of white Mississippians who accepted institutional racism as a natural, even divine, social reality because their parents and grandparents, teachers, ministers, newspaper editors, and political leaders had drummed it into them from their births. Some of these were militants who were willing to use violence to preserve segregation. And, for the most part, Ole Miss students were also numbered in Barnett's legions, though they looked at events in 1962 with ambivalence. On the one hand, most embraced segregation, but on the other hand, they were unwilling to defend it at the risk of jeopardizing their education.

So this is a story of individuals fighting for conflicting purposes within a social context that both fueled and limited their respective struggles. While Meredith charted his own course, his actions took him inevitably into the larger civil rights fight. Officers and members of the state NAACP, lawyers from the National NAACP Legal Defense Fund, students in the Freedom Rides of 1961, and activists at Tougaloo College in Jackson all, directly and indirectly, supported his desegregation challenge at Ole Miss. And while Governor Barnett acted out of his own convictions, which included both a commitment to racial segregation and a pledge to avoid violence, he operated within a culture that aided his fight to keep Ole Miss segregated but at the same time threatened a firestorm of violence.

This is a story of continuity as well as change. The Battle of Ole Miss in 1962 is the pivotal moment in the narrative, and as such, it represents a moment of profound change. Yet, what Meredith did that year continued a long tradition of courageous African Americans who dared challenge Mississippi's segregated universities. And, yet, the Battle of Ole Miss was but one battle—albeit, a very important one—in an ongoing war. Much has changed in Mississippi since 1962, but much has also persisted in a state where racial attitudes have deep roots.

The book seeks to tell these stories within the lived past, that is, the past as it unfolded, not the remembered past of the present. The risk of a presentist perspective is that of turning historical persons into one-dimensional figures who appear as the personification of moral absolutes. This story is not about James Meredith, the paragon of virtue, and Ross Barnett, the embodiment of evil. They, and all the other men and women who appear in the book, were fully human, driven by self-interest as well as lofty principles and tugged in multiple directions by numerous groups who wanted their respective champion to behave in a certain way. White Ole Miss students, activist segregationists of the Citizens' Council, and black college students and Civil Rights workers often displayed ambivalence in the face of crisis. While present-day viewers often see past actions with great moral clarity, to those living in that time circumstances were ambiguous and events contingent. In trying to decide what to do, Ross Barnett, for instance, was confronted by legal, constitutional, political, religious, personal, and historical questions. James Meredith was also pulled in many directions—by family, legal counsel, and the Kennedy Administration, as well as by the thousands of well-wishers and hate-mongers who flooded him with letters. All of the men and women in the battle for Ole Miss took their stances without knowing the outcome, acting out of myriad expectations and emotions, including those of hope, faith, and fear.

The book is organized in two parts—Part One: The Mississippi Way and Part Two: Confrontation at Ole Miss. Part One consists of Chapters 1–4 and explains how the parties arrived at the encounter of 1962. It provides context for understanding the respective experiences of growing up black and white in Mississippi and the rise of the early civil rights movement in the state and the countermeasures white Mississippians took to defend segregation and reassert white supremacy. Part Two, consisting of Chapters 5–8, begins with the court battle between James Meredith and the state and then describes the riot on campus when he arrived to begin classes in late September 1962. It ends with a look at Meredith's experiences as the only African American student on a hostile campus and an assessment of the results of this critical historical encounter.

....

PART ONE

The Mississippi Way

....

CHAPTER 1
....

Growing Up Black in Mississippi

....

The past is a foreign country: they do things differently there.

J. P. Hartley

....

Moses "Cap" Meredith drove his team of mules up the lane and stopped in front of the farmhouse. He had come for his cows, which had been grazing in the farmer's field as they had each spring and summer for the past several years. Today was the day that he would pay the farmer for grazing rights, retrieve his cattle, and take them back to his own farm to fatten them for market. Stopping before the walkway that led to the front porch, Cap remained seated and shouted out the farmer's name to make his presence known. There was no response. Cap knew that the farmer was at home, and, indeed, the man soon appeared at the doorway and hollered for Cap to come around back so they could talk. But Cap did not budge; he continued to sit in stony silence. Minutes stretched into an hour and then into three hours. The farmer was the first to tire of the stand-off, so he emerged from the house, and the two men conducted their business.[1]

What was going on in this seemingly strange encounter? Could it be that two adults lapsed into childish behavior: hollering at each other, waiting each other out? Or, was there bad blood that we do not know about? More than anything else, what explains this strange and potentially explosive confrontation is the racial identity of the two men and the setting of their encounter. Cap Meredith was black and the farmer was white, and their exchange took place in Mississippi in the 1930s. The white man expected Meredith to adhere to the racial conventions of segregated Mississippi and show deference to the white man by coming to the back door. In a state where white supremacy was ingrained in its citizens from birth, no self-respecting white would greet a black person at the front door; to do so would suggest that all Mississippians were equal and that race did not matter. In Mississippi during the 1930s, race most assuredly did matter. At every turn, blacks were reminded that they were second-class citizens. They lived in separate and usually shabby neighborhoods known to whites as "nigger quarters." They attended "colored" schools, where their textbooks were outdated and worn-out discards from white-only schools. They worshiped in their own churches, banned from white churches by vigilant deacons and elders. And, they entered white homes through the backdoor.

By violating that racial convention, Cap Meredith crossed a line, and in Mississippi blacks were killed for lesser violations of the racial code. Indeed, in the previous 50 years, Mississippi whites had lynched more blacks than did their counterparts in any other southern state: a total of 462, or more than 50 per 100,000 blacks. Lynching could be justified by all sorts of reasons, including such trivial acts as arguing with a white man, insulting a white man, and demanding respect from a white man—any of which could have been leveled against Cap in this instance. We do not know why the white farmer did not bring charges. Perhaps it was because he valued the economic relationship that generated revenue from Cap. Maybe it was because of Cap's solid reputation among whites as well as blacks in the county.

Cap's refusal to go to the back door is especially important because his son James witnessed it. Just a lad of seven or so, James had accompanied his dad that day. He looked up to his father, literally—Cap was over six feet tall—and figuratively—Cap represented what it meant to be a man. So James watched Cap's every move and listened to his every word. This particular episode was a painful lesson for James because during the three-hour wait he had to pee and his dad refused to let him leave the wagon and go into the nearby woods, lest the white man misinterpret the act as a sign of weakness. Upon reflection, James learned two important and enduring lessons that day. First, he understood that there was a racial code imposed upon blacks that governed every aspect of social behavior. And, second, he learned that, despite that code, Merediths did not regard whites as superior and refused to cringe before them in fear. On that and other occasions, Cap made it clear to James and his nine siblings that they must never debase themselves by going to the back door of a white person's house.

To understand James Meredith is to understand the world in which he grew up. In fact, he came of age in two places, and both shaped his character. First, he grew up in Mississippi, or more precisely, black Mississippi, where blacks were considered inferior, denied access to a decent education, barred from the best jobs and professions, segregated into shabby houses in run-down neighborhoods, and kept in their place by state-sponsored and vigilante terrorism. Such conditions taught blacks not only to fear whites but to grapple in deeply personal ways with their blackness in a society that saw black as less than white. But, second, James also grew up on his father's farm. There, under Cap Meredith's guidance, he rejected the world shaped by white supremacy and segregation and came to see himself and his family as a special people. As an adult, he recalled that perspective: "In Attala county Mississippi there were white people of every category from the highest to the lowest—from the richest to the poorest. There were Black people—good ones and sorry ones. And then there were the Merediths. We were a separate world."[2]

James was born on that farm in Attala County in 1933. Located in the Hill District of central Mississippi—a designation that Meredith applied to all of Mississippi lying outside the rich, fertile Delta—the farm was reached by driving northeast of Kosciusko on the old Natchez Trace, turning off onto a gravel road for a few miles, and then driving up a lane to the farmhouse. Cotton was the cash crop on the 84-acre farm, which also produced corn to feed the livestock—cows (both for milking and for fattening for market), hogs, and chickens. There was also a large vegetable garden. Cap Meredith took pride in being able to provide for his family by raising most of the food consumed on the farm and generating sufficient cash for other necessities. While he forbade his wife and children to work in a white woman's kitchen, he did on occasion approve of his wife taking in white folk's laundry for additional cash. There was plenty of work for all on the farm, including James, who from an early age was expected to perform chores such as carrying water to his father and older siblings during

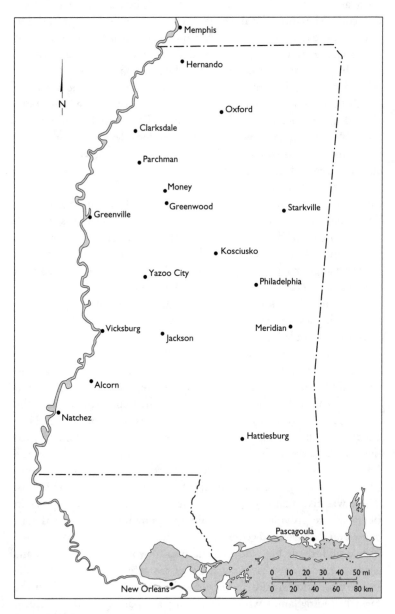

Map of Mississippi.

cotton-picking time. The farm had to be productive in order to meet the needs of a large family. Cap had two sets of children: one from his first marriage, which ended when his wife died, and another from his second marriage to James' mother.

At a time when the vast majority of blacks worked as sharecroppers, tenants, or farm laborers, Cap's position as a yeoman farmer afforded him and his family a degree of autonomy unknown to most African Americans, not only in the state, but in the country. There was little about Cap Meredith that was typical of black Mississippians, and one did not have to look far to understand his exceptional status. The first sign was the mailbox that marked the entrance to the lane leading to the farmhouse. A nameplate on the box read: "Moses Meredith, Rte. 2, Box 10." Few blacks owned post office boxes, and fewer still had nameplates. The second sign that Cap's family was unique was the house itself. It was a large dwelling with 11 rooms, far bigger than the shotgun houses that dotted the countryside in Attala County. The third sign was not visible from the farm; one would have to travel to the courthouse in Kosciusko to see it. There on the voting lists one could see the name of Moses Meredith, who had registered in 1925 and who continued to be one of the few black voters in the county until his death in 1965.

The cultural values that Cap instilled in his children were inspired by the land that he owned. While the modest farm, though larger than the average 53-acre farm of 1930s Mississippi, had no name posted at its entrance, the Merediths always referred to it as "my own place," to signify their pride in land ownership. Indeed, pride and order were at the center of the family culture. Order meant that everything on the farm was to be kept in good repair and placed in its proper place. That order could be seen in the house that stood on a hilltop at the end of a half-mile drive that connected to the gravel road. Compared to the houses of other Mississippi blacks, it was a mansion, though compared to houses of Mississippi whites, it was a rather shabby, ramshackle dwelling. But, as James remembered, there was always "paint of some quality on the outside" and there was "some kind of furniture in every room."[3]

Before he became a landowner, Cap had been a sharecropper, and, therefore, he treasured the independence that came with owning property. Sharecropping in Mississippi was a form of peonage that kept blacks in debt to landowners. It was a precarious existence that constantly threatened the cropper's freedom. With no land of their own, sharecroppers worked someone else's land and received a share of the crop for their labor. Most croppers began in debt and remained there. Without sufficient cash to pay for the necessities that they could not produce with their own labor, blacks had to borrow money from white storekeepers, often the landowners who were their landlords. Throughout the cotton-growing season, blacks purchased goods on store credit, and white storekeepers kept records of this book credit in their ledgers. After the cotton was picked, there was a reckoning of accounts. First, the cotton was weighed by the landowner on his scales. Then the cropper's share was determined by multiplying the weight by the price, and the price was set by the gin operator, who was sometimes the landowner and always a white man. From the sharecropper's gross proceeds, the storeowner deducted the amount of goods advanced to the cropper during the year, and the landowner deducted any amounts advanced to the cropper from various expenses such as medical treatment. Often the net amount showed a negative figure, that is, a balance that the cropper still owed his creditor. Under state law, debtors could be arrested and then fall under the forced-labor act passed by the legislature. The effect was the imposition of a form of slavery on the debtor as payment of his debt. Once in prison, the debtor could be leased to landowners in need of farm laborers. The system was subject to all sorts of abuses, including the imprisoning of black men and women for such minor offenses as vagrancy or for various trumped-up charges.

One victim of this prison gang labor system was Gransbill Williams, who recalled his experiences as a member of a prison labor gang. He remembered that while imprisoned at the state penitentiary at Parchman, "we were usually shackled to twenty- to fifty-pound iron weights." He added, "Those were very hard times. There was so much humiliation. And sometimes death." Williams recalled one member on his labor gang who had been arrested merely for associating with the "wrong" people. He also told of a 16-year-old girl who had been tortured and raped by the police at the time of her arrest. Williams said that escape was virtually impossible and that medical care was nonexistent. He spoke of the horrors of "shackle poison," an infection caused by the constant rubbing of ankle irons on the legs of prisoners,

a condition that sometimes resulted in a painful death. Anyone trying to escape was "put into a coffinlike sweatbox, beaten, or riveted
to twenty-five to fifty-pound iron weight shackles. The same thing
happened if we did not work hard or fast enough."[4] Historian David
Oshinsky noted that about 70 percent of the prisoners at Parchman
were black, and, generalizing on the kinds of brutality described by
Gransbill Williams, called Parchman a place "worse than slavery."[5]

Other blacks were tenant farmers who went to great lengths to
avoid the prison labor gangs. One of the strategies for staying out
of debt was for every member of the family, including the children,
to contribute to the family coffers. Chalmers Archer, Jr. grew up in
Lexington, located about 30 miles west of the Meredith farm, and
he knew the importance of marginal income for his family. "Under
these conditions," he wrote in reference to the severe segregation of
Lexington in the 1940s, "money was always a matter of grave concern
for blacks. Money other than what could be made from regular crop
sales was always needed but extremely hard to come by. For younger
blacks, making money to supplement the family income or for themselves was even more difficult. Therefore, making ends meet on the
farm was terribly hard when income from crop production did not
cover rent, food, mortgages, or other essentials." Daughters and wives
of black families often did maid's work for well-to-do white families
in the area. Black boys hired themselves out to do yard work for white
families. However, Chalmers' father, like Cap Meredith, forbade his
son from doing such work because of its degrading nature. "In those
days," Chalmers' explained, "no matter what the age of white children
in those families, blacks were required to address them as Mister or
Miss, and Papa always said that this act had caused many black youths
to develop feelings of inferiority. Thus, these odd jobs were not worth
the small amount that we kids might have made." However, the need
for money was so great that Chalmers' father consented to his peddling
fresh fruits and vegetables door-to-door in white neighborhoods. But
in order for him to peddle goods, he had to figure out how to avoid the
humiliating custom that relegated blacks to the back doors of white
homes, with the front doors reserved for white guests only. Chalmers found that the best approach was to ask anyone he found outside,
especially kids or maids or other black workers, to ask the homeowner
to come to the door. At times, he found that whites were angered to

find that a young black peddler had summoned them to the door, but they usually bought something anyway. With pride he added, "Who could resist our homegrown bounty?"[6]

Unlike Chalmers, James Meredith had little contact with whites. Whites owned the farms that surrounded Cap's farm, but most were far enough away to prevent daily encounters. The closest house was about a hundred yards behind the Meredith farm, separated by a fence and shielded by woods. The white owner leased the place to a black family, and the children of that family were James' best friends and playmates. Because Cap would not allow his children to play at other people's houses, all play took place on the Meredith side of the fence. Perhaps because he had so little contact with other children, James became something of a loner. He was an imaginative and reflective boy, who was quite capable and content to entertain himself. And in his first six years, he did so in a world where encounters with whites were limited.

Other black children growing up in Mississippi developed childhood friendships with white children, and those childhood friendships often ignored race. That was the experience of Anne Moody in Centreville in rural southwest Mississippi, where she and her family lived as the only black family in a white neighborhood. Anne's mother was a domestic working for white families, and the Moodys lived in a two-room house nearby. Anne remembered how she as a 7-year-old and her two younger siblings made friends with white children. The Moody children were playing "Indian" one day, beating tin cans with sticks and making war whoops. Their noise attracted the attention of some white children, two girls and two boys. Anne showed the newcomers how to emulate Indians; in turn, the white children showed her and her siblings how to skate and ride bicycles. That encounter and exchange was the beginning of what Anne described as a memorable childhood friendship. Although unaware of a racial divide between her and the white children, she did recognize a class difference. Her new friends lived in a nice house and had a playhouse that was nicer than any house she could have dreamed of living in.[7]

Charles and Medgar Evers had a similar experience growing up in Decatur, a town located about 60 miles south-southeast of Kosciusko. They played with white kids as small boys. Charles remembers their names: Margaret and Bobby Gaines, the Hollingworths, Sonny Boy

Jordan, and Johnny Keith. Like kids do everywhere, there were the occasional arguments and scraps, but never because of race. "Kids left alone," Charles reflected, "are beautiful that way," adding, "we ate together, swam together, slept together. Peas in a pod." But things changed around the eighth grade. The white kids stopped playing with the Evers boys. The kids were no longer "left alone" to decide matters of friendships and social interaction; through parents, church, school, culture, and law, they had gotten the message that people are not all equal—some are white and superior and others are black and inferior. That is when the Evers learned that they were "niggers."[8]

Although more isolated than most black children, James Meredith nevertheless lived in a society saturated with racial difference and could not avoid encounters with racism in the countryside around the farm. The largest landowner in the county lived on the road to Meredith's house, and James observed the demeaning treatment of blacks there. The farmer had an extensive operation, including timber, cattle, and farming, and he hired black laborers by the day to perform the myriad jobs. He required the workers to call him "Cap'n Sam," and he often amused himself by hitting the "niggers" with the heavy walking cane that he carried with him. On other occasions he tossed nickels and pennies in the air and watched the Negroes fight over them.[9]

Segregation came into sharp focus for James when he went with his family to Kosciusko on Saturdays to do the weekly shopping. In Meredith's boyhood, Kosciusko was typical of small market towns and county seats in Mississippi. Built on a square around the courthouse, the town's four sides housed all of the business and professional services for the community, such as banks, lawyers' offices, drug stores, general stores, and specialty shops. While African Americans spent most of their time on outlying farms or in the town's "colored quarters," on weekends they "went to town." Though white merchants welcomed the "colored trade," they maintained strict racial boundaries, such as separate rest rooms and water fountains, labeled "Whites" and "Colored." Some businesses, such as restaurants and cafes, were reserved for whites only. However, the central shopping district of town was also a place where whites and blacks came into contact with each other. Unwritten codes governed that contact. When walking on the sidewalks that linked the stores and shops, a black person of any age, upon meeting a white person, again regardless of age, had to step aside even if that meant stepping off the sidewalk entirely. Verbal exchanges were also governed by racial conventions. Whites called a black man "Boy" even if he were white-haired and stooped with age. Blacks used "Sir" or "Mister" in addressing white males, including boys, and they used "Ma'am" or "Missus" in addressing white females, including girls. Any contact between black men and white women, no matter how innocent, was of special concern to whites, who had a horror of blacks' "violating" "their" women. Fear of black men sexually "violating" white women had been ingrained in southern history and culture from the time of slavery. White male subjugation of blacks included sexual exploitation of black women and, at the same time, protection of "chaste" white women from the "bestial" desires of "over-sexed" black men.[10] Such attitudes lingered in Mississippi during the 1930s. As an adult, Meredith remembered Kosciusko's town center as a racially and sexually charged site:

> The town [center] was also the chief place of contact between the poor white men and the Negro women. The rich or well-to-do whites had more convenient means by which to satisfy their desires for a black woman. The white woman has long been considered the main object of conflict between the whites and the Negroes. I can assure you that the greatest point of friction between the races has not been the white woman; rather, it has been and still is the colored woman.[11]

As a young boy, Charles Evers discovered what it meant to be a "nigger" in Mississippi at the most basic level. Reflecting upon segregation in his hometown of Decatur, he defined it as a system designed by white folk to "keep us 'niggers' in line," and to illustrate he recounted a vivid description of just what that "line" meant:

> You knew you were a nigger the very first time you rode in a car, couldn't use the bathroom at the service station, and had to relieve yourself in the woods just off the road, hiding from passing cars. One day when I was nine years old, in uptown Decatur, I had to pee real bad. At a service station, I asked for the bathroom. A white man yelled at me, "We don't have no nigger toilets!" I knew he didn't like me, but I couldn't believe he'd forbid me to use his toilet. I thought maybe he hadn't heard me. I asked. "Can I just come in and pee?" He shouted, "No!" I peed all over myself, walked home, and asked my

parents why I couldn't use the gas station toilet. They said, "White folks are like that."[12]

In poignant detail, Evers described the many things that reminded a young boy that he was black and inferior in segregated Mississippi. He said, "you knew you were a nigger" when you started driving and older Negroes gave you the rules of the road: avoid the highway patrol and never let a white man pass you after dark lest he run you off the road or shoot you. He said that "you knew you were a nigger" when restaurants would not serve you and hotels would not allow you to spend the night or "even get a cup of coffee." Whites reminded Negroes daily that they were "niggers." If a black person went to a white's house, he or she had to go to the back of the house—never would they enter through the front door, even though whites would walk through the front door of a black person's house, often without knocking. Newspapers reinforced racial stereotypes daily: "the good that Negroes did was never mentioned, and the evil that whites did to Negroes was never mentioned." In Charles Evers' words, "White folks told us everything black was dirty, stupid, and dishonest." Moreover, they insisted that "God planned it that way." Popular culture, especially movies and magazines, depicted whites in the most flattering light and blacks in the darkest.[13]

In segregated Mississippi, whites called the shots and, in doing so, kept blacks off-balance by presenting two faces to blacks. On occasion, there was a "sweet closeness" between blacks and whites that touched Charles Evers as an endearing trait of his native state. Mississippi whites and blacks relate countless stories of acts of individual kindness in which whites were gracious to blacks and blacks were kind to whites. Yet, the fact remained that it was a world in which blacks had to dance to the white person's tune, sometimes literally. Medgar and Charles Evers' mother would on occasion send them to Charlie Jordan's store for sugar or flour. The two young boys dreaded going because Jordan would make them dance in front of the white men who hung around his store, calling out, "Dance, nigger!" On the other hand, the opera diva Leontyne Price, born in Laurel, Mississippi, in 1927, recalls that when a white family for whom her aunt worked as a maid learned that the maid's niece could sing, they helped pay her way to Juilliard and traveled to New York for her debut. Yet, as Charles

Evers put it, "that smiling face was a side of white folks that kept us confused."[14] Such individual acts of kindness described by Price and Evers were expressions of racial paternalism that belied the structural reality of the Jim Crow South.

Segregation in Mississippi was institutionalized and memorialized. Since 1911, a Confederate Monument stood on the courthouse grounds at Kosciusko as a proud reminder for whites that their forefathers had fought bravely against overwhelming odds to defend the Mississippi Way of Life, at the center of which were white supremacy and racial segregation. Theodore Bilbo was the governor of Mississippi when Meredith was born, and he constantly reminded Mississippians of the evils that attended race-mixing and miscegenation. Bilbo was a racist firebrand and published his views in a book entitled, *Take Your Choice: Separation or Mongrelization* (1946). He maintained that any race mixing would contaminate the purity of the races and would lead to the decline of each. He did not hesitate to speak for blacks in stating that the majority of "them" did not want race-mixing either. While many blacks did voice a preference for a segregated society, they still wanted equality of opportunity. While whites claimed that black schools, for example, were "separate but equal," blacks knew better. But, to Bilbo, blacks were inferior, and nothing good could come from their race. When Richard Wright, born in Roxie, Mississippi, published his autobiography, *Black Boy*, in 1945, Bilbo, then a U.S. Senator, denounced the book from the floor of the Senate, calling it an attempt to plant the seeds of "troublebreeding" and "devilment" in the hearts of Negroes. But, he concluded, "it comes from a Negro, and you cannot expect any better from a person of his type."[15]

White Mississippians like Bilbo did not hesitate to state with confidence what black Mississippians felt and believed about the "way of life" in the state. Citing their cooks, maids, and yardmen, whites never tired of pointing out that blacks really were contented with their place in segregated Mississippi, that they preferred it to integration elsewhere. Such a view was a delusion, a fiction to reinforce deep-seated convictions. African Americans knew differently. Writing in *Black Boy*, Richard Wright discussed the delusion: "The white South said that it knew 'niggers.' . . . Well, the white South had never known me—never known what I thought, what I felt. The white South said that I had a 'place' in life. Well, . . . my deepest instincts had always made me reject the 'place' to which the white South had assigned me." Lyrics of a Mississippi blues song captured the dual mind of blacks: "Got one mind for white folks to see, 'nother for what I know is me; He don't know, he don't know my mind."[16]

James Meredith's own search to know his mind began when he entered school. He began his education at age six in a school built by his father. Cap Meredith believed that education was the path to a better life for black children, a life with more opportunity and less drudgery. But there was no school near the farm, so Cap raised funds among blacks and built one. State and local officials exhibited no interest in providing for the education of black children. Governor James Vardaman (1904–1908) expressed the thoughts of many white Mississippians: "In educating the negro we implant in him all manner of aspirations and ambitions which we then refuse to allow him to gratify. It would be impossible for a negro in Mississippi to be elected as much as a justice of the peace.... Yet people talk about elevating the race by education! It is not only folly, but it comes pretty nearly being criminal folly. The negro isn't permitted to advance and their education only spoils a good field hand and makes a shyster lawyer or a fourth-rate teacher. It is money thrown away."[17] Of course, blacks saw thing differently. To them the "separate but equal" system was grossly unjust. In a 1918 appeal to the legislature, a group of blacks put it this way: "We cannot understand by what process of reasoning that you can conclude that [it] is humane, just or reasonable to take the common funds of all and use it to the glory of your children and leave ours in ignorance, squalor and shame." Expenditures on education confirmed their view. In 1950, the state spent four times the amount per pupil on white children as compared to black children.[18]

Chalmers Archer's educational experience in Mississippi confirmed the reality of separate and unequal schools for blacks and whites. He attended Ambrose Vocational High School in Lexington, and despite its being housed in an overcrowded building, "Ambrose did a surprisingly good job of student training." However, it was never intended to be an academic school because "[b]lacks in Mississippi...were not thought to need an academic high school, because they were not supposed to be intellectually capable of absorbing anything but vocational training." He noted that the school's physical condition remained substandard until the 1950s after the Supreme Court overturned the separate but equal doctrine. Then the state built better schools for black children. Archer remembers having to walk three and one-half miles to school, almost a mile farther than he would have needed to walk if he had attended the all-white Lexington High School. Even when Holmes County began providing bus service for school children, only white students could ride. School buses passed right in front of the Archer home to pick up two white children who lived about a half mile beyond, but they did not stop to pick up the Archer children. One superintendent of education made a point of announcing that "you blacks will never ride those yellow buses."[19]

Nor, as Archer discovered, would blacks receive an education that would equip them to compete with whites. First, he pointed out, the purpose of educating black children for whites in the Delta was to prepare them for the demands of a sharecropping economy, which meant that little attention was devoted to the three Rs. Second, books were outdated and substandard. Archer recalls his "falling-apart, hand-me-down history books from white public schoolchildren." The practice was for the state to adopt new textbooks for white children every few years and send the old ones to black schools. Archer noted that blacks had been virtually erased from the history books. "We found no information about black people," he wrote. "There was nothing about black artists, writers, scientists, political leaders, or military heroes. Unless we learned about them at home or directly from our teachers, we had no role models to admire and emulate."[20] Charles Evers had similar memories. No one talked about the contribution of blacks in building the country, North and South, or about the fact that blacks had died in the American Revolution for the very freedoms that they were denied.

Charles Evers recalled with clarity and pain the history lessons he learned from his textbooks. In his view the books "lied" about Reconstruction, pointing out that it was a disgrace, a time of federal violation of states' rights and a time of political corruption. Evers later realized that it was indeed a time that "had its troubles," but it was also a time when newly freed slaves had some hope for a better life. But, black southerners saw their hopes dashed when Reconstruction ended in 1877, leaving blacks with few economic resources while subjecting them once again to white rule. In other words, the failure of Reconstruction helped explain to black Mississippi students that their inferior place in society was not just an act of God or nature, but the deliberate denial of the constitutional guarantees of "equal protection of the laws" and "due process of the law" to American citizens of African descent. But, Evers declared, "I surely didn't learn that in the Negro schools in Mississippi."[21]

While still in elementary school, James Meredith transferred to the Negro school in Kosciusko because blacks in the county could not afford to provide a decent education at the school Cap built. But, James saw little improvement in his new school. He later wrote, "When I left [the Kosciusko] school in 1950 I had never been able to use a toilet because there was none, and I had never had a teacher with a college degree." White legislators did not value education for blacks who, they believed, were best suited for manual labor as agricultural laborers or as domestic workers. Nonetheless, blacks did value education. Meredith noted that "[o]ften the Negro high school principal is the number-one Negro in a Mississippi community. In the South education has almost become a religion since the days of Booker T. Washington. The Mississippi Negro will almost concede anything and sacrifice everything to get an education." He attributed the poor quality of education in black schools to segregation, not to the teachers, who "taught what they knew in the winter for thirty or forty dollars a month, saved most of it, and went away in the summer to learn something to teach the next winter, that is, if they found a school in the state to attend."[22]

While Mississippi students, white and black, learned little or nothing from textbooks about racial injustice and the struggle for civil rights, black children learned important lessons outside school, from events reported in the media and from instruction at home. Chalmers Archer recalled how in 1939 the Daughters of the American Revolution, a patriotic organization devoted to preserving America's heritage, refused permission for Marian Anderson, an African American contralto, to sing in Constitution Hall in Washington, D.C. The DAR owned the segregated building and would not violate its commitment to segregation to allow Miss Anderson to perform. In protest, Eleanor Roosevelt resigned from the DAR and helped arrange an open-air concert at Lincoln Center, where Marian Anderson performed before an audience estimated at 75,000. That event was cause for celebration among the students at Ambrose Vocational High School in Lexington. They spent almost two class periods discussing what it meant and the importance of identifying with persons like Miss Anderson.[23] Radio was an important means of expanding James Meredith's education. His father listened to the national news every evening, and James remembered hearing the broadcast of Joe Louis' first championship fight in 1938. In the Meredith household, Joe Louis represented hope and pride in fighting one's way to the top.

Meredith's most formative lessons, especially those regarding history, came not from school books, but from the ancestral history taught by his father. While James read the white-written and white-washed history textbooks that celebrated the Mississippi way of life, including racial segregation, he received an entirely different view of the past at home. It is that history that goes a long way in explaining young James' views of race and power. He viewed himself as atypical among Mississippi blacks because, according to the family history he had learned from his parents, he was part of a proud people who had descended from noble and even royal breeding. Cap Meredith taught his son that his lineage included that of African royalty and that his great-great-great-grandfather had been the last legitimate ruler of the Choctaw nation before whites under Andrew Jackson confiscated their Mississippi lands and forcibly removed them west of the Mississippi River. Meredith not only learned those family history lessons well, he developed a perspective on race that set him apart even from other blacks. Rather than considering himself as a member of an oppressed race trying to climb up, he deemed himself to be a member of a superior people. Moreover, Cap impressed on him that he had a duty and even a divine calling to restore his family to their rightful place.

At age 14, James began to make his aspirations known. To the dismay of one of his schoolteachers, he announced that he was going to attend the University of Mississippi. The teacher was appalled and frightened. Ole Miss, as the university was known, was all-white, and no black had ever enrolled there. For a black to even talk of going to Ole Miss was dangerous. White politicians had provided an alternative college for African Americans: Alcorn A&M, the state's all-black college, and to his teacher, that was where James should go. But, to James, an Ole Miss degree was but the first step in a much more ambitious plan to earn a law degree, practice law in Mississippi, and become governor of the state. He knew that most Mississippi politicians were graduates of Ole Miss Law School, so Ole Miss was the key to his plans. Teenagers often dream big, and James was no exception. While his teacher thought his plans were ill-conceived, he saw them as a mission.

Despite such lofty conceptions, the reality of Mississippi posed much grimmer prospects for Meredith and his classmates when they left school. While blacks constituted a little more than 50 percent of the state's population in the 1930s, they commanded but a tiny fraction of its economic resources. Most Mississippians, of both races, struggled to make a decent living. Per capita income in the state was the lowest in the United States, just 32 percent of the national average. But, Mississippi's African Americans were the poorest of the poor. In the decade of Meredith's birth, more than 80 percent of all Mississippians worked in agriculture, with only 56,268 manufacturing jobs available in a population that exceeded two million. Land ownership was the basis of wealth, and land tenure in Mississippi for blacks was about one-fourth that of whites.[24] Blacks were far likelier to work as wage laborers or tenants on white-owned farms than to work their own land.

Mississippi's segregated educational system and economic inequality went hand in hand. White children could take college preparatory courses, attend all-white colleges, enter graduate and professional programs, and take their place at the head of the professional and political life of the state. Colored children received just enough education to be useful workers in Mississippi's agricultural fields, where the majority worked, and do the physical labor in the state's business establishments. The only professions open to blacks were teaching and the ministry. The number of black lawyers and doctors in the state was miniscule.

What then was an aspiring young black person to do? One option was to join the exodus of blacks that left the state. That is what three of James' older siblings did in the early 1940s as the United States entered World War II. They went to Detroit and found jobs in factories that needed battalions of workers to meet wartime production goals. But leaving the state for northern factories did not fit James' plans. Neither did staying on the farm.

Cap wanted more for his son than Mississippi was willing to give him. So, just as he had refused years earlier to go around to the back door to do business with his white neighbor while James looked on,

Cap refused to settle for the educational scraps the state threw his son. He believed in James and, rather than dissuading him from following his dreams, sought ways to help him attain them. So, before James' senior year, Cap arranged to send his son to St. Petersburg, Florida, to live with Cap's sister and attend high school there. Though the school was segregated, it was far superior to the Kosciusko school. Most of the teachers had college degrees, and some had advanced degrees. Thus, in 1950, James Meredith left the state. Ironically, it would be in leaving Mississippi that James Meredith would discover a way to find opportunity within the state.

CHAPTER 2

....

Growing Up White in Mississippi

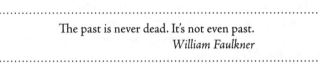

The past is never dead. It's not even past.
William Faulkner

For his thirteenth birthday, Willie Morris got the gift of his dreams. On a crisp autumn day, November 29, 1947, his parents took him to Starkville, Mississippi, for the annual football classic between Ole Miss and Mississippi State. This year was special because Willie's two favorite players would go head-to-head in the contest. Tom "Shorty" McWilliams was State's star player, a triple-threat tailback in the single-wing formation. He had transferred from the United States Military Academy at West Point, where he had received All America recognition while playing in the same backfield as the great Doc Blanchard and Glenn Davis. Charlie Conerly led Ole Miss. He had first entered the university in 1941, but left shortly after the Japanese bombed Pearl Harbor. After fighting on Guam and Iwo Jima during World War II, he returned to Ole Miss and became an outstanding passer, runner, and punter. Ole Miss was Willie's favorite team, and this season had been particularly thrilling because the Rebels were on top of the powerful Southeastern Conference. When Willie played touch-football back in his hometown of Yazoo City, he imagined himself scoring the winning touchdown for Ole Miss. The Rebels gave Willie the best present he could imagine: a 33-to-14 victory that resulted in the school's first undisputed Southeastern

Conference Championship. And, to top it off, both McWilliams and Conerly were brilliant.

Like James Meredith, Willie Morris dreamed of attending Ole Miss, a desire no doubt heightened that day in Starkville when he saw the Rebels in their glorious victory. Unlike Meredith, no artificial barriers stood in his way, so he could expect his dream to become reality when he graduated from Yazoo City High School. Morris was white, and growing up white in Mississippi meant access to the best education the state had to offer, and following graduation from college, positions of power and influence would be open. While attending high school over the next four years, his dream moved closer to reality. He was a bright, witty, energetic, and imaginative student who excelled in a wide range of extracurricular activities from editing the school newspaper to playing football, basketball, and baseball. As he thought of his future, he had his heart set on joining Mississippi's educated gentry, and an Ole Miss degree would help make that dream come true. At Ole Miss, he would be joined by his best friends, and afterwards they would return to Yazoo City and take up lives as Mississippi gentlemen in a place they loved.

That place was a world apart from James Meredith's world. But just as the Hill District and Black Mississippi shaped Meredith, the Delta and White Mississippi shaped Willie Morris. He was born in 1934 in Jackson, but grew up in Yazoo City on the southern edge of the Mississippi Delta, a flat stretch of rich farmland wedged between the Mississippi and Yazoo Rivers. Though now protected from flooding by levees that run along the 200 miles from Memphis to Vicksburg, the Mississippi had for centuries deposited layer upon layer of silt that had once been topsoil on midwestern farms, making the Delta one of the nation's most productive agricultural regions. Large plantations with hundreds, and often thousands of acres dominated the landscape. During fall at cotton-picking time, the land, when viewed from a distance, was a dazzling sea of white shimmering in the morning light. But from the perspective of black sharecroppers picking the fleecy fiber from stubborn, prickly bolls by hand, the land represented an endless round of backbreaking work that required constant bending while dragging a long cotton sack that grew ever-heavier as the day wore on. And at the end of the day, the croppers had little reward to show for their efforts, and they trudged off to their cramped, rundown houses that often stood in the midst of the dusty cotton fields.

But the Delta was more than a geographic region, it was a cultural zone, a place that author James Cobb called the "most southern place on earth."[1] In the words of writer David Cohn, it began in the lobby of the Peabody Hotel in Memphis and ended at Catfish Row in Vicksburg and captured the contrasts of Mississippi where gracious antebellum plantation homes graced the landscape in and around such towns as Yazoo City, Greenwood, Indianola, Greenville, Drew, Marks, and Clarksdale. Not only did cotton make the Delta the richest section of the state, it made its richest inhabitants the most powerful in the state legislature. While the Delta conjures images of mint juleps and southern belles, it also was the birthplace of the blues, that soulful music that came out of African American experiences in a land that for them took so much and gave so little in return. Composed while working in fields or relaxing at night, the lyrics speak of hope and frustration, love and rejection, and pleasure and pain.

Writer and former editor of *Harper's Weekly*, Willie Morris captured what it was like to grow up white in Mississippi. He lived in Yazoo City, a Mississippi town located at the southern end of the Delta, where the past cast long shadows over his childhood. Born the year after James Meredith's birth, Willie experienced life in a town that offered its white children encouragement, safety, and opportunity. He attended elementary school in a big old two-story structure with white columns, tall windows, and iron fire escapes that was situated on a three- or four-acre campus. When Willie and his classmates stood in front of the building, they could see the public library standing on one side of the campus and the gray Confederate monument looming over the opposite side. On top of the monument were two figures: a lady holding a Confederate flag and a soldier holding a rifle with a bayonet attached. When students entered the building, they saw portraits of George Washington and Jefferson Davis, the former the Father of the United States and the latter the Father of the Confederate States of America. Upstairs in the assembly hall where the students gathered each day, they took their seats facing the stage, which was flanked by the American flag on the right and the Confederate flag on the left. In class, the students learned about their heritage and its heroes,

including John Hancock, whose bold signature symbolized the patriotism of the early Patriots, and Robert E. Lee, Stonewall Jackson, Jeb
Stuart, and Nathan Bedford Forrest, who had fought to preserve the
southern way of life.[2]

As a young boy in the small town at the bottom of the Mississippi Delta, Morris experienced a life that was similar yet profoundly
different from that of James Meredith. Certainly the racial and social
landscape of Yazoo City was similar to that of Meredith's Kosciusko,
but Morris resided on the white side of the line, while Meredith was
on the black. For Morris, that meant that he attended school in the
segregated Free Public School System of Yazoo County, Mississippi.
Black kids in town attended an all-black high school designated simply as "Number Two," an apt appellation for a school that was clearly
second-rate in comparison to the white school. Like most young boys,
Willie noticed the difference between the schools by comparing the
equipment and appearance of the respective athletic teams. Known
as the "Black Panthers," the Number Two football players played in
the discarded uniforms of the white high school, which meant that
the two schools had the same colors—red, white, and black. Though
their colors were the same, players on the town's two high school teams
who wished to play football in college had different prospects. Morris
and his friends played countless hours of sandlot football in Yazoo
City dreaming of the glories of being gridiron heroes for Ole Miss
in games against Tennessee or other Southeastern Conference teams.
He grew up listening to Ole Miss football games on the radio, games
that he and his friends reimagined in their rousing games of tackle
in which they became the star running backs breaking loose for the
game-winning touchdown. Southeastern Conference football was a
source of immense regional pride for the young Morris, who listened
to the scores on Saturday afternoons, first enduring the results of
games from such little schools in the East like Amherst and Colby and
Niagara, then listening to those from the Ivy League, whose games
he regarded as mere exercises, and finally hearing the ones that really
mattered, those from the big southern powers.

More than the culture of a particular region within the state,
the culture of the state itself—the Mississippi Way—shaped white
Mississippians. Trent Lott illustrates that whites growing up in the
hardscrabble Hill District, as well as those in the Delta like Willie

Morris, also came of age in a culture where race predominated. Born in 1941 in Grenada, about 60 miles from Kosciusko in north-central Mississippi, Trent Lott, like James Meredith, spent his childhood in Mississippi's Hill District. Though living in neighboring counties, the two boys grew up in different worlds. It was not the distance that defined their divergent experiences; rather, in segregated Mississippi, it was race. A comparison of how each grew up illustrates the difference between growing up black and growing up white in Mississippi.

Grenada and Kosciusko were similar towns in the 1940s and 1950s; each was a county seat; each was a market town for surrounding farmers; each had populations about equally divided between whites and blacks; and each was segregated. Because race was the most important factor in determining the world that a young boy or girl would experience growing up in either of the two towns, it would not have mattered which town each called home. James Meredith grew up on the black side of Kosciusko, while Trent Lott grew up on the white side of Grenada. Neither had a choice in determining his race, and yet his race determined the boundaries within which he would live. As individuals, the boys were quite similar; they were smart, industrious, and ambitious. Both were determined to use their talents to attain lofty and similar aspirations. As young teenagers, each dreamed of becoming a lawyer and making a difference in Mississippi, and each viewed an Ole Miss education as essential to his success.

Unlike James Meredith, Trent Lott did not grow up on a place that his family could call their own. Rather, his father Chester worked two jobs to support his family; he was a pipe fitter and a sharecropper, tilling some 20 rented acres with a borrowed mule to supplement his income. Trent's mother Iona was a schoolteacher. Lott situated his family among the town's "blue-collar" workers and subsistence farmers. In a memoir published in 2005, Lott characterized his family as "rock-solid," possessing a strong work ethic. Despite hard work, the Lotts lived in somewhat straitened financial conditions, although, Trent noted, he never felt for an instant that he and his family were poor. In fact, they were like most white folks in Mississippi at the time; they worked hard but had very little to show for it. With few rich people in the state, everyone was in a similar economic state and thus surrounded by people of like circumstances. With pride he recalled that he and his parents always comported themselves with honesty and integrity, paying their bills and attending church.[3]

The Meredith family in Kosciusko was also a hard-working clan that paid its bills and attended church each Sunday—neither the Lotts nor the Merediths looked to anybody but themselves for their living. In his memoirs, Lott expressed a sentiment that not only described his family's values but no doubt that of the Merediths as well:

> I don't have much sympathy for people who don't work to help themselves; I don't think the government owes you a living. My parents didn't get any government help, and they never had fancy jobs. Even though there were times when they didn't have enough money, they never thought of running to the government the way everybody does now.... I know I sound like a Southerner. Well, I am, and I'm proud of that, too.[4]

James Meredith and his father would have agreed with those sentiments, including the regional pride. Of course, they were opposed to the racial politics based on white supremacy, but they loved the South and they loved Mississippi. They certainly subscribed to Lott's notions concerning hard work and independence.

Lott's discussion of the role of the federal government in the lives of Mississippians points to an important contradiction within the white Mississippi conservative mentality. On the one hand, Mississippi politicians like Senator James O. Eastland constantly thundered against federal government intrusion into state affairs, most particularly those regarding matters of race relations. He opposed "welfare" payments that he said discouraged poor blacks and whites from working hard and pulling themselves up by their bootstraps. At the same time, however, Eastland voted for and received huge federal subsidies to sustain his enormous delta plantation in Sunflower County. In 1967 alone, Eastland received a $168,524.52 subsidy for cotton price supports and acreage reduction.[5]

Up to this point in the comparison between James Meredith and Trent Lott, if race is kept out of the picture, the story is one with many parallels. But, their stories diverge sharply when Lott describes his family's place in Mississippi politics. Meredith's family was outside the state's political society. They were ineligible to hold any political office, even at the local level. But, Trent Lott grew up in Mississippi politics. He came from what he called a "fabled Mississippi family that was well schooled in politics." In the late nineteenth century, his uncle John Lott, who had lost a leg at Gettysburg, ran for Mississippi state treasurer but was soundly beaten. His maternal grandfather was a justice of the peace and his maternal grandfather was a supervisor of Carroll County. Thus, Lott wrote, "In a sense I grew up with politics." As a toddler he attended political rallies. And, from the age of seven or eight, he could not get enough of the frequent political conversations among the family politicians. His family, like nearly all white Mississippi families in the 1940s and 1950s, was Democratic. His dad was a "yellow-dog" Democrat, one who had spent his lifetime voting for his party's slate of candidates, even if the candidate happened to be little better than a "yellow-dog."[6]

Like most other white Mississippians, Trent Lott and Willie Morris learned about the Mississippi Way the same way that blacks did: through state-adopted texts. But those lessons, especially on the subject of race, were reinforced by the broader culture. Ole Miss history professor James Silver studied the indoctrination of Mississippi youths in the 1950s and noted that, with few exceptions, they gave "unconditional and unswerving" acceptance to the doctrine of white supremacy. This unquestioning attitude rested on an interlocking sequence of what Silver called "discredited assumptions":

a. the biological and anthropological "proof" of Negro inferiority
b. the presumed sanction of God as extrapolated from the Bible
c. the present state of affairs as one that is desired and endorsed by Negroes and whites alike
d. the repeated assurance that only through segregation can law and order prevail
e. a view of history which declares that there has been a century of satisfactory racial experience in Mississippi
f. a constitutional interpretation which denies the validity of the Supreme Court desegregation decisions[7]

Newspapers also reinforced the doctrine of white supremacy, and both Lott and Morris were avid readers. Writing at the end of the 1960s, Hodding Carter, editor of the *Greenville Delta Democrat-Times*, noted the role of the Mississippi press in reinforcing the southern interpretation of history. He pointed out that the antebellum press helped condition southerners to resent all criticism of the South—first that coming from abolitionists, then that from all northerners. Then, during Reconstruction, the southern press worked for the white primary as a tool for disenfranchising blacks, and it promoted and reinforced the concept of "solidarity of a white South, that would brook no question, even by a friend." He concluded that "a hundred years after the end of the [Civil War], the earlier conditioning would bring the old response."[8]

Thus, white Mississippians grew up reading in their local newspapers articles and editorials that confirmed suspicions engendered by their history texts that the federal government, as well as all "outside agitators," were bent on destroying the southern way of life. The list of "outside agitators" over time expanded far beyond carpetbaggers and scalawags to include Communists, liberals, union organizers, the National Association for the Advancement of Colored People (NAACP), all civil rights workers, the U.S. Supreme Court, and, in 1962, the Kennedys.

With few exceptions, Mississippi's churches supported racial segregation and white supremacy as derivative, not only of natural law, but of divine law. Trent Lott was a member of the Southern Baptist Church, and Willie Morris was a Methodist. Both boys attended church regularly with their mothers, while their fathers seldom attended. At Sunday school they learned lessons on race that echoed those in their school texts. While subscribing to biblical teachings of the brotherhood of all men and the equality of all "under Christ," Mississippi's Protestant churches for a hundred years after the Civil War seemed to be more obedient to the strictures of white southern culture than to biblical commandments. Indeed, throughout that period the three largest denominations bore regional designations: the *Southern* Baptist Convention, *Southern* Methodists, and *Southern* Presbyterians. These churches were born during the antebellum period and defended the southern political stance. Moreover, the church in Mississippi played an important role in justifying the institution of slavery and in supporting the decision for secession. Dominated by evangelicals who thundered about the need for personal salvation but said little about social injustice, Mississippi was and is part of the so-called "Bible Belt" that extends across the South, and white ministers interpreted the Bible through a distinctive southern and racist lens. While early in the nineteenth century individual preachers spoke against slavery, by the 1840s and 1850s ministers were solidly behind the "peculiar institution." At first they justified human bondage on the grounds that it was a "necessary evil," that Mississippians had never enslaved anybody but had merely purchased men and women and children who were already enslaved. Besides, they argued, "they" were better off under the benevolent care of slave owners in Mississippi than under the warlords of West Africa. Moreover, for many, their enslavement was the instrument of their spiritual salvation; without slavery they would continue to live in a "benighted" land of superstition instead of in the light of Christianity.

In the 1950s, the Citizens' Council, an organization that began in the Delta town of Indianola and was dedicated to preserving white supremacy, politicized religion in defense of segregation. Recognizing that segregation had widespread appeal among Mississippians, but always concerned about any weakening of that conviction, the Council published a series of pamphlets arguing that segregation was not only the Mississippi way but also that of orthodox Christianity. Quoting scripture that had formerly been used to defend slavery, the Council sponsored such titles as "A Jewish View of Segregation," "A Christian View on Segregation," and "Is Segregation Unchristian?" The Council propaganda taught that segregation was "God's own plan for the races." Segregation was "a holy thing" embodied in the law of God. Racial mixing was, in the words of one minister who espoused Council views, "a violation of God's natural law in Creation." He asked, "Do black birds intermingle with bluebirds? Does the redwing fly with the crows?" In the Council's interpretation, American history supported biblical teachings and natural law. In one of its history lessons, the Council stated, "If we are bigoted, prejudiced, un-American,... so were George Washington, Thomas Jefferson, Abraham Lincoln, and our other illustrious forebears who believed in segregation."[9]

White youngsters in Mississippi viewed African Americans through a wide spectrum of views and emotions, moving between moments of affection, pity, and excitement, on the one hand, to those of contempt, disdain, and cruelty, on the other. Those feelings derived from unequal relationships in which the white person, even if younger and less experienced in life, was always the superior, whether the relationship was that of a black nanny and her charge, a black worker and the son or daughter of his or her employer, or simply that of a casual acquaintance made over lines drawn on buses or in waiting rooms or on the streets. But, as Willie Morris observed about Yazoo City, "the broader reality was that the Negroes in the town were *there*: they were ours, to do with as we wished. I grew up with this consciousness of some tangible possession, it was rooted so deeply in me by the whole moral atmosphere of the place that my own ambivalence—which would take mysterious shapes as I grew older—was secondary and of little account." Reflecting on his boyhood attitudes toward African Americans, Morris wrote, "My own alternating affections and cruelties [toward blacks] were inexplicable to me, but the main thing is that they were largely *assumed* and only rarely questioned."[10] Negroes were simply part of the landscape that whites inhabited and, for the most part, were objects to be seen and used, not subjects to be regarded as fully human.

Unlike Morris, Richard Rubin did not grow up in Mississippi. He was a New Yorker who lived for about a year as a journalist in nearby Greenwood. Nonetheless, he, too, like the native whites, realized that he could choose when and if to think about blacks at all. Explaining how segregation shaped his assumptions, Rubin wrote:

> After all, I lived in a white neighborhood. I ate in white restaurants. I worked in a white office, had a white job, and availed myself, consciously, or not, of the uncountable advantages and privileges and opportunities and freedoms afforded me solely because, yes, I was white. But the truth was that, as obvious as it was to … everyone else in town, up until that moment I had never thought of myself that way; I'd always enjoyed the luxury of not having to think about it at all.[11]

The character of race relations in Mississippi was often reduced to stereotypes. Though many whites could point to deep and sometimes lasting friendships with individual African Americans, they often referred to members of the Negro race in derogatory terms. For example, most whites would not think of calling an African American friend or acquaintance a "nigger," but white Mississippians freely referred to blacks in general as "niggers" or, perhaps, "nigras." From the 1940s through the 1960s, especially as the civil rights movement sought to break down segregation, whites refused to use the more respectful term "Negro" in speaking of or to blacks. But white attitudes went beyond the use of words. White youngsters learned as a matter of course, from every part of their society, that there were certain negative behaviors and conditions inherently associated with being a "nigger." Willie Morris put it this way:

> "Keeping a house like a nigger" was to keep it dirty and unswept. A "nigger car" was an old wreck without brakes and with squirrel tails on the radio aerial. "Behaving like a nigger" was to stay out at all hours and to have several wives or husbands. A "nigger street" was unpaved and littered with garbage. "Nigger talk" was filled with lies and superstitions. A "nigger funeral" meant wailing and shouting and keeping the corpse out of the ground for two weeks. A "nigger store" was owned by a white man who went after the "nigger trade." There were "good niggers" and "bad niggers," and their categories were so formalized and elaborate that you wondered how they could live together in the same town.[12]

Trent Lott and Willie Morris, like most Mississippians, grew up in small towns, and the intimacy of those places ensured that their social and racial attitudes did not venture far from community norms. The state could boast of no large cities; the capital Jackson was the only city with a population of 100,000 or greater, and it barely exceeded that number in 1960. Few other towns numbered as many as 40,000, and the vast majority had populations under 20,000. Living in small towns meant that white youngsters grew up in face-to-face societies where they knew most other whites and where they were widely known. Small towns tend to promote conformity, and certainly that was the case in Mississippi, especially regarding attitudes and behavior toward race. African Americans were accepted, tolerated, and sometimes befriended, as long as they stayed in their place. Urban culture with its diverse cultural offerings lay outside the state. Indeed, the saying in the state was that Memphis and New Orleans were Mississippi's two largest cities, and, indeed, Mississippians flocked to those two cities for a taste of culture that could not be found at home. Ironically, that culture included the rich offerings of African Americans: Memphis was home of the blues and New Orleans home of Dixieland Jazz.

No place in the state more symbolized white Mississippi than did Ole Miss. For its students, race imposed no boundaries on white Mississippians; indeed, it defined social preserves for privileged whites. Not only was Ole Miss the oldest state school, it boasted the state's only law school and medical school, thus, providing most of the state's professional and political leaders. Indeed, Governor Ross Barnett was a graduate of the law school, and he was determined to maintain the university as a white-only institution. The other state universities at the time were more specialized institutions: Mississippi State University was an agriculture and mechanical institute; Mississippi Southern College was a teachers college; and Mississippi State College for Women was an all-women's liberal arts college.

Most Ole Miss students were Mississippians, and most would stay in Mississippi after graduating. In a state where the majority of young people, white and black, did not go to college, they were the privileged few. Located on the edge of the Mississippi Delta, Ole Miss in the early 1960s represented the best and worst of Old South culture and tradition. The campus itself evoked a strong sense of place and time, especially among its students and alumni. With a nod toward William Faulkner, what Mississippi historian David Sansing says about southerners applied to Ole Miss students as well: they "don't learn about their past, they absorb it." Reminders of that past abounded from the Lyceum, where wounded Confederate soldiers were treated, to a cemetery a thousand yards to the east, where some 700 of the Civil War fallen, both blue and gray, were buried. One visitor noted that "history still overwhelms this campus like kudzu. The streets are named Confederate Drive and Magnolia Lane. The students are called Rebels."[13]

Ole Miss in the 1950s was arguably the most southern college in the country. Located at Oxford on the northeastern edge of the Delta, the school reflected the region's social and cultural heritage. The academic year began with a "Welcome Rebel Party" in the fall and ended with "Dixie Week" in the spring. Many fraternity and sorority houses looked like colonnaded plantation homes found in the Delta. Confederate flags were everywhere: draped across dormitory windows, hung from balconies, and waved by the thousands at football games. The marching band played stirring music that evoked

Confederate statue on the Ole Miss campus.
From the collection of Robert D. Loevy

regional pride. The school's alma mater began, "Way down South in Mississippi...." And the strains of "Dixie" followed the playing of the national anthem and always got a louder reception.

Trent Lott no doubt spoke for many Ole Miss students when he described his visceral attachment to Ole Miss as a place of beauty and history. In his memoirs, he recalled a strong sense of place when he first arrived on campus as a student. He said that from the beginning, he was "in thrall of the colorful pageant that is Ole Miss." To him it was a pageant rooted in a past that was so much a part of Mississippi, from before the Civil War to the present. He wrote, "I instinctively felt the history that suffused the place." In words that conjure thoughts of Plato's Academy in the olive groves of ancient Athens, Lott singled out "the Grove" as the one spot on campus that captured the spirit of the campus and its students. It was there among the graceful hardwoods, he remembered, "where alumni and students greeted each other at homecomings and other campus celebrations," thus forging and renewing bonds between existing and future leaders in the state.[14]

White Mississippians, most of whom never walked on the Ole Miss campus, basked in the favorable national publicity that the university attracted in the 1950s, especially that accorded its highly ranked football teams. Indeed, on game day one could readily see white Mississippi reflected in the crowd. Willie Morris observed, "Delta cotton money is present among the sunburnt old boys in khakis and overalls." The air was filled with rebel yells and "Hotty Toddys," a popular school cheer, and Mercedes mingled with pick up trucks.[15] Regardless of their circumstances, they lustily cheered a winning team in its glory years of the 1950s and early 1960s. By any measure, Ole Miss boasted one of the nation's premier football programs. In the 10-year period ending with Meredith's graduation in 1963, the team, under the direction of Head Coach Johnny Vaught, won five Southeastern Conference championships, finished in the top 10 national rankings 7 out of the 10 seasons, played in 8 bowl games (winning 6), and was named national champions in 1959. SEC football was a source of regional pride for southerners, and Ole Miss football was a source of state pride for Mississippians. Vaught tapped into that state pride in recruiting the state's best athletes and in cultivating fan support. Vaught explained the connection: "Boys we get from out of state can go home and never hear about Ole Miss football," he says. "But in Mississippi the game is talked about all year round. We like to get Mississippi boys, boys who love Ole Miss and want to win for her."[16] Ole Miss football was a way of expressing southern manhood on a national stage, demonstrating, at least to southerners' satisfaction, that their young men could defend the state's honor with a virility that reflected that of their Confederate forbears.

But Ole Miss symbolized more that the fighting spirit of Mississippians. It represented the beauty, grace, and gentility of southern womanhood. Ole Miss coeds were recognized nationally as being as beautiful as the football team was powerful. Willie Morris, like many other observers, called the women at Ole Miss the "most beautiful coeds in America," again reflecting a time when more attention was given to women for their beauty than their brains. In 1959, Mary Ann Mobley of Brandon was named Miss America, and in 1960 Lynda Lee Mead of Natchez was crowned as her successor. When Meredith entered Ole Miss in 1962, Miss Mississippi, Miss Missouri, and Miss Tennessee were students. For many Mississippians at the time, the Miss America pageant represented the best of white womanhood, a womanhood that was best preserved in an all-white institution.

Of course, the university boasted about its academic standing as well. There, however, the case was more difficult to make. By most standards of measurement, Ole Miss was not a distinguished seat of learning. It could not claim an outstanding faculty of national and international standing, nor could it say that its admissions policy winnowed out all but the brightest students. Its library holdings were modest at best. School boosters could and did point to a high number of Rhodes Scholars coming from Ole Miss, bragging that no university in the South could match the number it had sent to Oxford.

The racial climate at Ole Miss in the mid-1950s is illustrated in two controversies. First, in 1955, the football team won the Southeastern Conference and was invited to play in the prestigious Sugar Bowl. However, what would otherwise have been an easy decision became complicated when it was announced that their opponent would be the University of Pittsburgh. Bobby Grier, an African American, was Pitt's star running back, and thus, to play in the Sugar Bowl meant that Ole Miss would play an integrated team. To elude controversy, Ole Miss decided to forgo the Sugar Bowl and accept an invitation to play in the Cotton Bowl against the all-white Texas Christian University. Some observers believed that university officials had engineered the Cotton Bowl invitation to avoid embarrassment.[17] Race had created a dilemma. On the one hand, devoted fans as well as players wished to take on all comers and play the Pitt Panthers. On the other, many on campus as well as throughout the state found it incomprehensible that Ole Miss as a public university would belie the state's commitment to preserving racial segregation by playing an integrated team.

The second controversy embroiled the students more directly. In 1955, University Chaplain Will Campbell invited Alvin Kershaw to campus to speak on religion and modern drama. A southerner from

Louisville, Kentucky, Kershaw was an Episcopal rector and philosophy professor at Ohio University. He had gained national notoriety when he appeared on the popular television program, "The $64,000 Question." After winning $32,000, he was asked what he would do with his winnings, and he indicated that he would probably donate a portion to the NAACP, a statement that set off a firestorm among some Ole Miss alumni. Chancellor John Williams received numerous letters from powerful graduates who insisted that he withdraw Kershaw's invitation to speak. However, the student body felt otherwise, believing that a university should be a place where all ideas were aired. In a poll conducted by the student newspaper, the *Mississippian*, about 80 percent of responding students thought Kershaw should come to the campus. However, when Kershaw later admitted that he was a member of the NAACP, a number of students joined alumni in urging that Williams withdraw the invitation. A petition to cancel signed by about 300 students expressed their desire "to link ourselves with the great mass of Mississippians desiring to uphold segregation in the State of Mississippi." Armed with such support, Williams withdrew the invitation. The controversy illustrates that free inquiry at Ole Miss was a victim of what historian Charles Eagles called the "closing" of Mississippi society in the mid-1950s.[18]

Ole Miss is the point of convergence for James Meredith, Willie Morris, and Trent Lott. Each aspired to attend the university, and each saw an Ole Miss degree as requisite for realizing his dreams of becoming a productive, influential citizen in the state. But in the 1950s, Ole Miss remained open to whites only, just as it had been since its founding in 1848. At various times, such as during Reconstruction, state and university officials feared that political pressure from outside the state would lead to integration, but none of those fears had led to the enrollment of a black student. So when James Meredith graduated from high school in St. Petersburg, Florida, in 1951, he did not consider applying to Ole Miss. To do so would have been folly at a time when he could count on no legal or government assistance to support his cause and ensure his safety. Instead, he postponed his college education and joined the Air Force.

On the other hand, Trent Lott and Willie Morris not only had access to Ole Miss, they had other choices available to them as well. Trent graduated from Pascagoula High School in 1959, where he was an outstanding student and a student body leader. His family had moved to the city on the Mississippi Gulf Coast when his father took a job in the shipyards there. In high school he developed a keen interest in law and knew that he wanted to become a lawyer. When he started thinking about college admissions, he made his decision based on the college's law school. He considered two universities: Tulane and the University of Mississippi. In his assessment, Tulane had several pluses: a "magnificent campus," a "reputation of attracting some of the best professors in America," and its location in New Orleans. But, the law school curriculum was based on the Napoleonic Code, which was the basis for Louisiana's legal code, but not that of any other state. The University of Mississippi made more sense to Lott's "practical mind." He explained that he wanted to practice law in his home state and it was only natural he study a form of law that would equip him for that goal. But there was more to his decision. He wanted "a Southern school with demonstrated success in [his] home state—one that nurtured young law school graduates and provided a support system as well." So, not only did he have a choice of where to attend college, he had access to the institution that he knew would provide all the support he could want in his chosen profession.[19] So, in 1961, Trent Lott drove the more than 300 miles north from Pascagoula to Oxford and became a freshman at Ole Miss.

Willie Morris made a different choice. In 1952, as he neared graduation at Yazoo City High School, he still had his eyes on Ole Miss. He was the class valedictorian, and his classmates voted him the most likely to succeed, and as he considered the future, he had a wide range of good options. His desire to fulfill his dream of attending Ole Miss had intensified that spring when he went to Oxford for a conference. While there he watched the filming of the jail scenes in the movie *Intruder in the Dust*, based on the book by William Faulkner, an Oxford resident. So he returned to Yazoo City confirmed in his plans to attend Ole Miss in the fall. Then one day just weeks before graduating, Willie's dad gave him some unexpected advice. He put aside the Memphis *Commercial Appeal* that he was reading and turned to his son and told him, quite simply, to "get the hell out of Mississippi."[20] Henry Rae Morris had long been critical of the Mississippi Way. He rejected the fundamentalism that characterized much of the religion in Evangelical Churches. And he thought that any taxpayer, black as well as white, ought to vote. He knew that if Willie went to Ole Miss and stayed in the state, he would likely never escape that stifling culture. Willie heeded his father's advice and decided to leave the state and attend the University of Texas at Austin. At the time he did not completely understand what was behind his father's advice, but he later regarded it as a gift far greater than the trip to Starkville five years earlier to see his beloved Ole Miss Rebels play football.

....

CHAPTER 3

Black GIs Challenge
"The Mississippi Way"

....

We've waited too long already.
Charles Evers

....

One day in 1946, Medgar and Charles Evers, recently discharged from the U.S. Army, went to the Newton County courthouse in Decatur to register to vote. The next day they announced their intentions to their family, and their father was worried for their safety, especially after the white clerk, Alton Graham, paid a visit to Mr. Evers and told him that if his sons did not want trouble they should forget about voter registration. Ignoring their father's concern and the clerk's warning, Medgar and Charles proceeded with their plan, but upon reaching the courthouse they encountered a crowd of whites who blocked the courthouse entrance. Graham addressed them, "Who you niggers think you are?" Charles replied, "We've grown up here, we fought for this country, and we think we should register." At that moment, the old county circuit clerk, a Mr. Brand, who knew the Evers family, shuffled over to defuse the situation. He was, in Charles' estimation, a decent man, who, like most Mississippi whites, did not want murder or bloodshed but did not dare help blacks secure their civil rights because they did not want to be branded "nigger lovers." Such persons would soon discover that they, as well as the blacks they wished to help, would be whipped, or worse. But Mr. Brand intervened that day in the only way he knew. He counseled Medgar and Charles

to be patient, to go home and wait for a time when whites were ame-
nable to black voter registration. He said, "the time will come when you
can register." Recalling his recent experience of crawling around in the
mud of New Guinea, Charles told Mr. Brand, "We've waited too long
already." Warning them that their persistence would lead to trouble, the
old man nonetheless let them register.[1]

The Evers brothers knew that registration was but part of the
battle in Mississippi; actually voting would be a bigger hurdle. As election day approached, Alton Graham paid another visit to the veterans'
father with a warning: "Your boys better not come vote, because we're
going to get them if they do." A steady stream of white bigots and black
"Uncle Toms" came by the house over the following days, each bear-
ing a similar message: do not vote or risk your lives as well as those of
other blacks. Former governor and current senator Theodore Bilbo
raved as the election neared and more and more black veterans across
the state had registered to vote. In his best race-baiting voice, he thundered, "The best way to stop niggers from voting is to visit them the
night before the election." Intimidation had worked in the past; Bilbo
was certain it would once more. On election day, Medgar, Charles, and
five of their friends went to the polls early to beat the crowd, but upon
arriving at the courthouse, they met about 250 "rednecks, dressed in
overalls, holding shotguns, rifles, and pistols." With a .38 in his pocket
and a switchblade in his hand, Charles led the small group of blacks
to the door. Again, old Mr. Brand scurried over to defuse the confrontation. "You Evers boys come from a good family," he said. "Why go
looking for trouble like this?...Charles, you and Medgar, you all go
back, you're going to cause trouble." Charles replied, "Let me tell you
something, Mr. Brand. We're going to vote—or else we're all going to
hell today. It's up to you. Now, give us our ballots." The six blacks then
split up to walk through the doors to get their ballots, but a knot of
whites prevented their entrance at each door. At one, Charles spotted a white man named Andy May, a "nice man" who owned a local
drugstore, whom Evers considered to be a friend. But, when Charles
greeted May with a pleading smile, the white druggist hissed at him like
a snake and patted the gun in his hip pocket. "Listen, nigger, ain't nothing happened to you yet." Coming from a "friend," those words stung,
but they also convinced Medgar that the whites were determined to
prevent them from voting even if it meant bloodshed. Deciding that

they would not prevail that day, the small band of blacks left the court-house. Whites shouted as they left, "You damn Evers niggers going to get all the niggers in Decatur killed."[2]

The Evers brothers were two of more than 80,000 Mississippi black men whose service in the military during World War II represented a fight for democracy around the world and a fight for social justice at home. Indeed, a program that enjoyed widespread sympathy among African Americans across the country underscored the war's dual purpose. In 1942, the *Pittsburgh Courier* launched "The Double V Campaign" (Double V), which called for "Democracy: Victory at Home, Victory Abroad." Throughout the war, the *Courier* remained patriotic, yet pushed for civil rights for blacks. The campaign always showed loyalty toward the war effort because the black press was sensitive to criticism for pushing its own agenda ahead of the national agenda. Nonetheless, black readers continued to link their own quest for civil rights with that of America's victory over fascism, evidenced by the title of one letter to the editor, "Should I Sacrifice to Live 'Half American?'"[3]

After the war, some of Mississippi's returning black veterans attempted to pursue the second half of the Double V campaign: victory over racial discrimination. Their army experiences had been a continuation of segregation; they had served in segregated units, lived in segregated barracks, and socialized in segregated clubs. However, despite the terrible experiences in a military regime that treated them as second-class soldiers, some blacks had glimpses of life beyond segregation—the possibility of living in a society that afforded all citizens equal opportunity. First, they had taken seriously America's war aim to make the world safe for democracy, to enable all peoples to live in freedom from tyranny. So when they returned to Mississippi and once again encountered entrenched racial segregation, they demanded the same freedom for which they had fought for others. But the freedom they sought was no abstraction. They wanted the chance for their children to get a better education. They wanted their children to grow up in a society where a hardworking person could earn decent wages without falling into debt. Also, many of the veterans had lived in other countries whose societies were integrated. In places like France and the Philippines, black soldiers had seen different racial environments than that back home, ones where skin color was less a factor among the population and where interracial relationships occurred with little outcry. There Mississippi blacks had mingled with whites in ways that were inconceivable back home. They had experienced integration first-hand and knew that it was entirely consistent with the principle of liberty and not the harbinger of all the social ills white Mississippians had for so long predicted.

What set Mississippi's returning GIs apart from tens of thou-sands of other black Mississippians who left the state was the fact that they came back. Moreover, many of them returned to fight for equal opportunity. Many other Mississippi blacks who rejected their inferior place in the segregated order simply fled and never returned. Between 1910 and 1960, almost a million African Americans emi-grated from the state. Their motives can be gleaned from the letters written to their contacts in the North. Economic conditions—crop failures, boll weevils, low wages, poor jobs, and lack of land—pushed them out. One woman from Ellisville stated, "Wages here are so low [we] can scarely live." A Hinds County man put it thusly, "Cap'n, I've been working here for a dollar and four bits a day and that's good wages for a nigger in Jackson. Flour is costing me nearly two dollars a sack, meat is so high I can't eat it. I am leaving because I can't buy food." In addition to citing hard times as a reason for leaving, black emigrants also cited discrimination, injustice, and violence. They talked about inferior housing and schools and the lack of opportunity for their chil-dren. So they left the state in search of a better place.[4]

When Charles and Medgar Evers came back to Decatur after the war, they discovered that while they had been changed forever by their wartime experiences, Mississippi had not changed at all. During the war they made money. In fact, Charles had saved $3,000, enough for his dad to add four rooms to their house, install indoor plumbing, and replace the wood stove with an electric stove. But, outside the house, the segregated society "seemed all stuck in the past." Much had hap-pened to the Evers boys. Charles had served in New Guinea and the Philippines and Medgar in France and Belgium. Each had romantic relationships that lingered after the war: Medgar with a "cute French girl" who wrote him letters and Charles with a "gorgeous" Filipino girl who wanted to marry him. Of course, both realized that they could not bring their girlfriends to Decatur, Mississippi. Their mother feared that just receiving letters from foreign girls was dangerous because if "scared white folks in Decatur would find out her boys were writing love letters to white girls," they might lynch them; they had lynched blacks before for far less.

Charles and Medgar broke off correspondence with their wartime lovers, but they could not slough off the deeper transformation in their attitudes toward themselves and society. As Charles put it, "Fighting World War II woke up a lot of Negro GIs, especially in the South." They had served in places that, compared to Mississippi, were "without racism." And yet, they asked themselves, if the United States was the world's greatest democracy, why were they "second-class citizens"? Why, they asked, could France have so little racism and Mississippi have so much? Charles summed up the reality that he and Medgar faced upon returning to Mississippi: "Medgar and I couldn't bring home to our free country the white girls who loved us overseas. And in our democratic country, we couldn't vote. Mississippi whites could kill us just for trying to do either one."[5]

In 1946, Medgar and Charles entered Alcorn Agricultural and Mechanical College on the GI bill. The all-black college was named after James Lusk Alcorn, a hot-tempered white man who after the Civil War could not stand the idea of returning black soldiers going to the University of Mississippi. So he led a movement to found a school for blacks. For the Evers brothers, Alcorn was the best choice the state had to offer. Ole Miss was still "lily-white," and Alcorn provided teacher training, thus enabling blacks to enter the one profession open to people of color in the state. However, Medgar and Charles did not fit in; most of the students were "country boys, green kids who just wanted enough schooling to make forty dollars a month teaching." The Evers brothers were among the few GIs on campus, separated by their older ages and by their experiences of fighting overseas. Charles thought that the education was all right "for a Negro school in Mississippi in 1946," but he resented the "false" depiction of Negro history taught there. He explained, "We used the same old white racist textbooks that described us as savages and Reconstruction as a terrible evil."[6] But Medgar and Charles applied themselves and enjoyed life. They made good grades and excelled in sports; Charles played center on the football team and Medgar played halfback.

The greatest lessons that the Evers brothers learned during their college years came outside the classroom, especially when they attempted to register to vote. They could not square the fact that they had fought for freedom and democracy, the country's founding principles, and yet they could not vote. The law said that they could vote, but white Mississippians made sure that they could not. Before the war young men like the Everses had endured racism without a fight, but returning veterans were tougher and prouder and not so easily swayed from claiming their rights.

While the day they were turned aside from voting was a humiliating and infuriating moment for Medgar and Charles, it also was an event that steeled them for future civil rights battles and represented a turning point in their lives. Charles later recalled the event and what it meant:

> Medgar and I never forgot that day. After risking our lives in a war for democracy and free elections, we had come home and were nearly killed for trying to vote. We were told that we weren't good Americans because we believed that all men are created equal. More than any other single thing, that day in Decatur made Medgar and me civil rights activists.[7]

Their bitter experience in being denied the fundamental right to vote only deepened the Evers brothers' determination to break down Mississippi's walls of racial segregation. But, they had to devise a different strategy, one that would close the gap between the rights guaranteed to all citizens under the United States Constitution and the systematic denial of those rights in white-controlled Mississippi. As their experience at the Newton County courthouse had confirmed, white Mississippians were not going to voluntarily grant equal rights and opportunity to blacks. But, they recognized that a direct assault on the entrenched political base of segregation would not work either, so they embarked on a long, slow, but relentless quest for equal opportunity for themselves and for all blacks in the state. They knew that if blacks were to be full and equal citizens, they must have equal educational and economic as well as political opportunity. And they believed that those rights could be won only through the federal courts and with a great deal of help from the federal government.

In 1948, while Medgar and Charles were still at Alcorn A&M, President Harry Truman had given them hope by issuing an executive order desegregating the nation's armed forces. Executive Order 9981 issued on July 26 declared that it was the policy of the president as

Commander in Chief "that there shall be equality of treatment and opportunity for all persons in the armed services without regard to race, color, religion or national origin." With that order, the president of the United States expressed his agreement with black veterans that those who fight for freedom and democracy are surely entitled to the fruits of their efforts. For Medgar and Charles Evers, Truman's policy meant there was now a federal model for the kind of society they envisioned, one where all were granted equal opportunity without regard to skin color.

Six years after Truman's historic decree, the U.S. Supreme Court handed down a decision that mandated with the rule of law the end to racial segregation in the nation's schools. On May 17, 1954, the justices in a unanimous vote overturned school desegregation in the landmark case, *Brown v. Board of Education, Topeka, Kansas*. Arguing for the plaintiffs, Thurgood Marshall, Chief Counsel of the NAACP, claimed that the Fourteenth Amendment, which required the states to provide equal protection under the law for all citizens, applied to public schools and, therefore, prohibited any school policy based on race. The U.S. Department of Justice in the Eisenhower Administration supported Marshall's interpretation, though calling for gradual implementation of the ruling. In his opinion explaining the Court's decision, Chief Justice Earl Warren declared that racial segregation in public schools was unlawful, that the doctrine of "separate but equal" schools was unconstitutional. A year later the Court, in what became known as *Brown II*, endorsed the Justice Department's notion of gradual implementation by calling for desegregation with "all deliberate speed." Nonetheless, for Medgar and Charles Evers, the *Brown* decision meant that federal law was now in line with their goals and aspirations.

Medgar soon learned, though, that federal law did not necessarily apply in Mississippi, where all schools from elementary through college remained separate and unequal. He and Charles graduated from Alcorn with what they considered to be the equivalent of an eighth grade education. Rather than accepting such injustice quietly, Medgar joined the fight to force Mississippi to comply with the *Brown* decision and offer all of its citizens equal opportunity.

Mississippi's nascent civil rights movement in the 1950s consisted of two organizations headed by a handful of courageous war veterans who were no longer willing to sit by and watch black men and women suffer for simply wanting to participate in democracy. Amzie Moore had been a corporal in the Army who spoke out against the contradictions of black soldiers fighting for rights that they were denied. In Calcutta he addressed a group of comrades who had been denied entrance to a segregated enlisted-men's club. Before the war he had not thought that much about segregation, but now it confronted him as a degrading reality: he could fight with white Americans against a common enemy, but he could not have a drink with his white counterparts. He recalled his thoughts at that stark contradiction: "Why were we fighting? Why were we there? If we were fighting for the four freedoms that Roosevelt and Churchill had talked about, then certainly we felt that the American soldier should be free first." While still in the service, Moore joined the NAACP, determined to fight for racial justice, a fight he continued when he returned to Cleveland, Mississippi, in 1946. There he confronted rising violence against blacks, a deliberate attempt, he thought, to intimidate returning servicemen. Undeterred, Moore became involved in organizing blacks, first, through the NAACP and, second, through a local organization founded in 1951, the Regional Council of Negro Leadership (RCNL). Based in the relatively safe, all-black town of Mound Bayou, the RCNL was a parallel but counter organization to the all-white Delta Council that enabled white people to speak with one voice on economic issues.[8]

The goals of the NAACP and the RCNL were twofold. First, they wanted to engage blacks in the political process through voter registration. Fewer than 10,000 of the state's almost one million blacks could vote in the early 1950s. Second, Mississippi civil rights leaders thought it was time to integrate the University of Mississippi. In 1953, E. J. Stringer, President of the NAACP State Conference on Branches, gave a speech underscoring the need for more black lawyers in the state, lawyers who could carry on the legal fight for civil rights. Ole Miss Law School was where most Mississippi lawyers were trained, so Stringer urged qualified blacks to apply there. Medgar Evers responded to Stringer's vision by applying for admission with help from NAACP counsel Thurgood Marshall, but over the protests of his parents and his wife Myrlie. Medgar moved forward in the belief that "the benefits of ... breaking down the barrier at Ole Miss" far outweighed the "immediate complications" that his application would pose for his family and for blacks in general.[9] For nine months the state deliberated over how to handle Evers' admissions attempt. White officials had no intentions of admitting a black to Ole Miss, but they wanted to base their rejection on defensible legal grounds. They knew that the federal courts were looking closely at southern states' efforts to deny fundamental rights to blacks. Ten years earlier, the U.S. Supreme Court had struck down Mississippi's white primary. Thus, with Evers' attempt to enter Ole Miss, officials at the highest level, including Governor James P. Coleman, sought a legal means of rejecting him. Finally they found what they deemed to be sufficient technical grounds for denial. University policy required two letters of recommendation from prominent citizens in the applicant's hometown. Medgar's letters had come from persons in Newton County, where he grew up, rather than from Bolivar County, where he was living at the time. The University decided that those letters were therefore invalid. Further, the University, in anticipation of future attempts by blacks to enroll, announced that henceforth applicants would need five letters of recommendation from alumni.[10] This new requirement was clearly a means to circumvent legal rulings without appearing to do so.

Upon receiving the rejection letter, Medgar immediately contacted Thurgood Marshall to file a lawsuit against the University on the grounds of racial discrimination. E. J. Stringer, however, persuaded Evers to drop the lawsuit and become the NAACP's first field secretary in Mississippi. He thought that Medgar could better serve the cause of civil rights in that capacity than by getting bogged down in a lengthy and uncertain court battle. Evers reluctantly agreed to give up his fight for a spot at Ole Miss and moved to Jackson. If he had harbored any notion that his life would be easier or that he and his family would be safer in his new position, he was soon disabused of those ideas. Shortly after he and Myrlie opened the office in Jackson, they received death threats from angry whites, something they anticipated, but what they had not foreseen was the lack of cooperation from professional blacks. Effectively barred from the legal and medical profession, black professionals were restricted to teaching in segregated schools and preaching in black churches. But when Medgar tried to enlist their support in the fight for civil rights, he found them reluctant to get involved. Their reluctance was understandable. First, some African Americans with professional or independent incomes had done fairly well for themselves under Jim Crow because segregation eliminated some forms of competition. Second, their fear was a logical emotion in Mississippi during the 1950s. Nevertheless, in 1958, Medgar expressed his frustration:

> As much good as the NAACP had done to make the opportunities greater for teachers who once made $20 a month and are making up to $5,000 [a year] now, we don't get their cooperation. The professionals are the same way. Only in isolated cases do they go all out to help us. Some ministers are almost in the same category. . . . [They] won't give us 50 cents for fear of losing face with the white man.[11]

Black activists in civil rights had reason to be afraid. Six months after the NAACP opened its field office, a local activist in Belzoni, Mississippi, Reverend George Lee, was murdered by a gunshot to his head while he sat in his car. Lee had protested recent acts of violence against black business owners in Belzoni. In April, whites smashed the windows of several black business establishments and automobiles to intimidate blacks who attempted to vote. In one instance, the terrorists left a note: "You niggers paying poll tax, this is just a token of what will happen to you."[12] Evers remembered the mid-1950s by the names of the victims of race-hatred: Ed Duckworth shot to death; Milton Russell burned; Charles Brown killed in Yazoo City; George Love killed by a posse; Jonas Causey killed in Clarksdale; William Roy Prather, a teenager, killed in a Halloween prank; Mack Charles Parker dragged from his jail cell and killed; and Emmett Till, a 14-year-old Negro from Chicago, dragged from his relatives' house, pistol-whipped, shot to death, and thrown into the Tallahatchie River.

The Emmett Till murder was particularly notorious and, because it attracted international publicity, became a rallying cry for Mississippi's civil rights movement. Emmett was murdered because he did what 14-year-old boys often do: show off for their peers. One day while visiting his cousins in Money, Mississippi, a tiny hamlet in the Delta, he taunted them because they went out of their way to avoid white people, especially girls and women. Emmett said that in Chicago things were different and bragged that he had had a white girlfriend. While the boys were in a small grocery store that catered primarily to sharecroppers around the town, someone in the group dared Emmett to say something to Carolyn Bryant, the white storekeeper who owned the establishment with her husband. What happened next is unclear. Emmett did not want to lose face, so he made some gesture. Mrs. Bryant said he said, "bye baby." One of the boys said he whistled. Either was sufficient to put him in grave danger in the Mississippi Delta. Carolyn Bryant told other whites, who were outraged and decided that such a breach of racial boundaries could not be tolerated. So on August 28, 1956, a small band, led by Carolyn's husband Rob, decided to "teach the boy a lesson." The lesson ended in a brutal beating that rendered the boy's face barely recognizable.

News of Emmett Till's murder evoked reactions of disbelief and outrage from persons all over the country and around the world. How could authorities condone such brutality against anyone, especially a 14-year-old boy? Like many young teenagers, he was guilty of showing off and making a tasteless comment, but he had committed no capital offense. Of course, he was accorded no right to protection under the law and given no opportunity to explain his side of the story. His mother later explained that Emmitt suffered from asthma and that she had taught him to whistle when his asthma acted up so as to calm him down and control his breathing. She suggested that he was no doubt nervous inside the store trying to look brave before his peers and might have started whistling to calm his fears. That, she thought, could have been construed as a wolf whistle. Whether or not one believes Mrs. Till's explanation, the point is that she was discussing a 14-year-old boy, not a hardened criminal.

The Till murder, in particular, represented a turning point in Mississippi's civil rights movement. First, it brought national and international attention to Mississippians' willingness to do anything to maintain racial segregation. Determined to put a face on Mississippi's racism, Till's mother, Mamie Bradley Till, insisted that gruesome pictures of her son's body be published throughout the world. And Medgar Evers took up the cause to shame all Americans with the story of Emmett Till. Whites mounted a trial of the perpetrators in an effort to counter the new publicity that threatened to force change. But it was a sham trial. The murderers were acquitted, which, as much as anything, was an indictment of the Mississippi justice system. Second, the Till case angered blacks and stiffened their resolve to resist white violence. Many attended the trial, some carrying weapons, and many more joined local NAACP chapters. Amzie Moore dates the beginning of the modern civil rights movement in Mississippi from that time.

Despite the rise in black participation in the fight for civil rights, blacks could not break the racial barrier that kept Mississippi's schools separate and unequal. Two cases illustrate the lengths to which state officials would go to prevent integration. The first case was that of Clennon King, a history instructor at Alcorn A&M., who in 1958 applied to the University of Mississippi for admission to the Graduate School to pursue a Ph.D. in history. He had high expectations for admission because he had a masters' degree from Case Western Reserve, and, more importantly, he had made public his views on race, which conformed to those of most Mississippi whites. Indeed, King had won the applause of Governor J. P. Coleman for a series of newspaper articles he had written in 1957 attacking the NAACP. In one of the articles, King said the organization was "negatively affecting race relations in the South" and suggested that the NAACP was in fact the "National Association for the Agitation of Colored People." Coleman might have liked such rhetoric, but King's own students found it repugnant. So angry were students at all-black Alcorn that they boycotted classes, vowing not to return until the administration purged the faculty of "Uncle Toms" like King.[13] After he left the faculty under pressure, King applied to Ole Miss with the expectation that whites would support his application. He claimed that whites had encouraged him to write the articles in the first place, and he noted their effusive praise. Governor Coleman stated publicly on television that King was correct in his characterization of the NAACP. So, when King applied to Ole Miss the following year, he was optimistic. He had sound academic credentials, and he thought he had the endorsement of high officials.

However, King underestimated the state's commitment to segregation, especially that of its premier university. When King appeared before the registrar at the Oxford campus, expecting to be admitted, he was taken aback to hear that his application had been rejected. He knew that his record made him a qualified and acceptable candidate, and he knew that his views on race and civil rights were in line with those of whites. So he was furious that he had been turned down because of his race. He was understandably upset and vented his anger and frustration to the registrar, who called for assistance to calm King down. State officials, who were on hand at Ole Miss for the occasion, quickly determined that King's reaction was symptomatic of mental instability. Accordingly, they arranged for a psychological evaluation, and as a result of that examination, the state committed him to the State Hospital for the Mentally Insane at Whitfield, just outside Jackson. Having arrived at Ole Miss to enroll in graduate school, King left to be locked up in a mental institution.[14]

The second case involved Clyde Kennard, who applied for admission to Mississippi Southern College in Hattiesburg. Born in Mississippi, Kennard left for Chicago at the age of 12 and graduated from Wendell Phillips High School. Like Medgar Evers, Kennard was an army veteran, having served as a paratrooper in the Korean War. After being discharged, he attended the University of Chicago but left after his junior year and returned to Mississippi to run his family's chicken farm after his stepfather became disabled. He applied for admission to nearby Mississippi Southern in order to finish his degree. Although Kennard had worked with the NAACP, he did not view his application as part of a desegregation crusade. In fact, he rejected any assistance from NAACP lawyers, thinking that if he made it clear that he was not a pro-integration militant but just a veteran seeking to complete his education that his admission would be granted. He hoped to appeal to the patriotism that he knew ran deep in Mississippi, where those who served in the military were held in an honored and exalted state. But, he underestimated an even more fundamental sentiment in the state: that of white supremacy and racial segregation.

In what can be described only as a Kafkaesque chain of events, Kennard found himself in the state penitentiary in Parchman for the next three years instead of beginning classes at Mississippi Southern. First, Governor James P. Coleman approached Kennard with an offer to pay all of his tuition and expenses if he would withdraw his application to Southern and attend instead one of the state's all-black colleges. After Kennard turned down Coleman's offer, maintaining that it was better for him to attend nearby Mississippi Southern so he could continue to operate the family farm, the state resorted to stronger measures against him. Determined to justify their rejection of his application to

Southern, state officials scurried about trying to find some basis for discrediting Kennard and, thereby, justify their actions on grounds other than race. In trumped-up charges, they accused him of receiving $25.00 of stolen chicken feed from the Forrest County Cooperative warehouse. Bringing a criminal case against Kennard solely on the testimony of one individual, Johnny Lee Roberts, the state sought to convict Kennard of a felony and then claim that his conviction proved that he was of low moral character and therefore should not be admitted to a state university. After deliberating for just 10 minutes, the all-white jury found Kennard guilty, and the judge sentenced him to seven years in prison to be served at Mississippi's notorious prison at Parchman. Medgar Evers attended the trial and afterwards, while fighting tears of outrage, called it the "greatest mockery of judicial justice."[15] Even some white newspapers in the state commented on the harshness of the sentence, but, nonetheless, Kennard spent most of the rest of his life in prison. While at Parchman, he was diagnosed with colon cancer, and after serving three years, he received a suspended sentence from Governor Ross Barnett, dying shortly thereafter.[16]

While Medgar Evers, Clennon King, and Clyde Kennard tried in vain to desegregate Mississippi's colleges, James Meredith was thousands of miles away at the Tachikawa Air Force Base in Japan. While in 1951 he had put on hold his dream of attending Ole Miss, the dream had never died, and recent events gave him hope of fulfilling it. He had followed in particular the news from Little Rock, Arkansas, in 1957 when nine black students attempted to enroll at the all-white Central High School. In compliance with federal law, the city of Little Rock had proceeded with plans to desegregate its schools, but Governor Orval Faubus blocked the attempt to integrate Central High. Though a relatively moderate and progressive governor, Faubus nonetheless recognized the Little Rock racial crisis as an opportunity for political gain.[17] Accordingly, he ordered the National Guard to surround the school and keep the black students from entering. Although a federal judge granted an injunction against the governor's actions and the guardsmen were removed, angry mobs threatened the black students' safety. When Little Rock Mayor Woodrow Mann asked for federal assistance in protecting the teenagers, President Eisenhower intervened by federalizing the National Guard and sending in 1,000 members of the Army's crack 101st Airborne Division under the command of Edwin Walker of the Arkansas Military District.

Meredith took hope from Little Rock. He had long maintained that Mississippi blacks could never break the state's segregated school system without federal government support. To him it was wishful thinking to hope that white Mississippians would voluntarily desegregate their schools, and the recent attempts by King and Kennard proved his point. But, if he could get the kind of support that Eisenhower gave the Little Rock Nine, Meredith thought he might yet realize his dream of going to Ole Miss.

However, when Meredith returned to Mississippi in August 1960 after being discharged from the Air Force, he deemed that, while conditions were hopeful, they were not yet favorable for him to apply to the University of Mississippi. Accordingly, he entered all-black Jackson State University in Jackson and awaited the outcome of the presidential race between Republican Richard Nixon and Democrat John Kennedy. Throughout the campaign, civil rights leaders across the country had urged Kennedy to take a more aggressive stance in support of civil rights, but Kennedy had worried that too strong a position would cost votes in the South, and the South, he reckoned, was crucial to his election. The South in the 1950s and early 1960s was the Solid South that had traditionally voted for the Democratic candidate. In Kennedy's calculation, the loss of the Solid South's electoral votes would be difficult, if not impossible to overcome. However, when Martin Luther King was jailed in Atlanta following his arrest on a traffic violation, Kennedy called his wife and Robert Kennedy called the judge. At the same time, Nixon decided to remain silent. Though he had made some attempts to reach out to Republican blacks in the 1950s, he had come to the conclusion that the black vote was already lost to the Democrats and that he might benefit from the growing disaffection among southern whites with the Democratic Party's support of civil rights, particularly the threat of desegregation in schools. Meredith took hope from the strong civil rights plank that Kennedy had insisted on at the recently concluded Democratic National Convention in Los Angeles. The party pledged to support full rights for blacks, including access to public schools. Moreover, the platform called for the end of tactics intended to delay implementing school integration as called for in the *Brown* decision.

Shortly after Kennedy's narrow election in November, Meredith decided that he would apply to Ole Miss. In his mind, Kennedy's election was essential to his strategy. He reasoned thusly:

> I was firmly convinced that only a power struggle between the state and the federal government could make it possible for me or anyone else to successfully go through the necessary procedures to gain admission to the University of Mississippi. I was also sure that only the recognition of the authority of the federal government would insure a successful completion of a course of study once admitted to the university. The election of President Kennedy provided the proper atmosphere for the development of such a situation. The strongest point in our favor was the civil rights platform which Kennedy insisted upon at the Democratic convention.[18]

Meredith was now ready to act. He had crafted his strategy much as a military leader would plan a campaign. He had benefited from fellow veterans in the state, in particular Medgar Evers and Clyde Kennard, whose forays had met with fierce resistance but had yielded valuable intelligence for future attacks. He had seen Mississippi's "closed society" brought under the spotlight of publicity in the Emmett Till case. He had watched the federal government commit its might on behalf of the students at Little Rock, and he was confident that the Kennedy Administration would do likewise for him at Ole Miss. And, he knew that there was a growing number of civil rights activists within the state who were prepared to take on the entrenched system of segregation. But, Meredith was under no illusions. He also knew that the state would mobilize the white community with all of its quasi-official organizations in defense of states' rights and racial segregation. He knew that he was in for a battle.

So did Medgar Evers. When Meredith came to the NAACP office in Jackson to seek legal counsel for what was sure to be a battle to enter Ole Miss, Evers questioned him closely. He wanted to make sure that Meredith understood the lengths to which the state would go to prevent his admission. Medgar knew firsthand what happened when a black man threatened a sacred racial boundary in Mississippi. No doubt he remembered that day in 1946 at the Newton County Courthouse when angry whites had threatened Charles and him with their lives for exercising their constitutional right to vote.

CHAPTER 4

Whites Mobilize Against the "Second Reconstruction"

Mississippi: The Closed Society
James Silver,
University of Mississippi History professor

When Clyde Kennard announced his intentions of entering Mississippi Southern College, Governor J. P. Coleman dispatched Zack Van Landingham, special investigator of the State Sovereignty Commission, to Hattiesburg to coordinate resistance. He first enlisted the services of reliable black informers who were willing to provide information on Kennard and try to persuade him to drop his enrollment plans. The lead informant was R. W. Woullard, a pastor and owner of an insurance company and funeral home, whom both the Forrest County sheriff and the Hattiesburg police chief deemed to be a "reliable black leader." In the past, Woullard had prevented an NAACP chapter from being organized in his church and had provided white officials with names of activists within the civil rights movement. So Woullard and three black school principals, whom Van Landingham also recruited, visited Kennard to persuade him to drop his plans. Kennard refused to back down. Next, Van Landingham turned for assistance to the local chapter of the Citizens' Council. He found the head of the Hattiesburg council, Dudley Conner, to be cooperative and even eager to assist. Conner volunteered that "if it was desired for Kennard to leave Hattiesburg and never return," the Council could "take care" of him. When pressed to explain what he meant, Conner suggested that, for example, Kennard's car could be hit by a train or he could have some other "accident," and nobody would ever know the difference. Such talk made Van Landingham nervous, so he rejected Conner's offer. He had hoped to resolve the matter peacefully, not with violence associated more with the Ku Klux Klan that with the governor's office.[1]

Van Landingham's efforts at stopping Kennard's challenge to desegregate Mississippi Southern reveal multiple levels of resistance. First, there was cultural resistance, which made all other forms of resistance effective. Cultural support for segregation and resistance to integration ran deep into every part of the Mississippi Way, including family and social life, education, religion, and media. Second, there was organized resistance orchestrated by state government. Van Landingham represented the Mississippi Sovereignty Commission, a state agency that reported directly to the governor. It was the state's watchdog for detecting and stopping any attempt to threaten segregation. Third, there was organized resistance at the grass-roots level. Dudley Conner was a member of the Citizens' Council, an organization of concerned citizens operating in every community across Mississippi to monitor public sentiment concerning segregation. The Citizens' Councils disavowed violence, Conner's sentiments notwithstanding, preferring instead social and economic pressure against those who showed the slightest support for equal rights. Finally, there was violent resistance. The Ku Klux Klan was a terrorist organization that operated with virtual impunity in Mississippi. Operating behind white robes and the black of night, the KKK burned crosses in front of the houses of black activists and their white sympathizers and followed that warning with violence that included burning houses and churches, kidnapping and beating those who did not heed the message, and, on occasion, killing those who persisted in fighting for civil rights. While the Klan operated outside the law, it enjoyed the sympathy of several Mississippi governors from the 1930s to the 1960s. The reality was that a governor would distance himself from the Klan while at the same time engaging in parallel activities that denied African Americans their rights.

While the *Brown* decision and Eisenhower's support of the Little Rock Nine heartened James Meredith, they infuriated Mississippi's white segregationists and galvanized them into action. As committed as Meredith was to breaking the back of white supremacy in order to enjoy his full civil rights, segregationists were as determined to fight for states' rights. To white Mississippians, states' rights was a sacred constitutional principle that viewed the states as equal, independent, and sovereign republics whose rights included all those not granted to the federal government by the U.S. Constitution. States' rights included, they argued, all matters pertaining to race relations and public education. When the federal government threatened the institution of slavery, a matter, according to Mississippians, for the states to decide, the state seceded from the Union and went to war rather than submit to federal "tyranny." Now the federal government was again encroaching on Mississippi's rights, and white Mississippians resolved to fight.

In 1954 the U.S. Supreme Court threatened the revered Mississippi way of life by declaring unconstitutional one of the linchpins of segregated Mississippi. The Mississippi Constitution rested on the principle of separate schools for blacks and whites, and state officials in the 1950s insisted that those schools were equal. The *Brown v. Board of Education* decision struck down "separate but equal" and called for the integration of public schools. Only by opening all schools to children of both races could blacks and whites enjoy equal opportunity for a quality education. Though the court gave states some breathing room in implementing the decision by ordering integration to proceed with "all deliberate speed," white Mississippians braced for a second Reconstruction, with the federal government once again dictating how their society should be structured.

Mississippi officials responded to the *Brown* decision by vowing to strengthen the state's segregated school system through what they called an "equalization" program. They conceded implicitly that white and black schools had been unequal, but they vowed to equalize them and thus give a lie to the Supreme Court's contention that separate schools were inherently unequal. No one gave much credit to the scheme, and the novelist William Faulkner thought it absurd. In a 1954 letter to the Memphis *Commercial Appeal*, Faulkner declared, "We Mississippians already know that our present schools are not good enough." He supported his claim by noting that annually those Mississippi young people who want "the best of education" leave the state. He could have been talking about bright students like Willie Morris. That was evidence enough for him that "our present schools are not even good enough for white people." So how could that system, he asked, if offered to black students in the "equalization" program, possibly satisfy the thirst of blacks who wanted quality education? He was appalled at the state's action: "We beat the bushes, rake and scrape to raise additional taxes to establish another system at best only equal to that one which is already not good enough."[2]

When James P. Coleman took the oath of office as Governor of Mississippi on January 17, 1956, he pledged that he would do every-thing in his power to maintain the "separation of the white and negro races" in the state. Despite the *Brown* decision and attempts of indi-vidual blacks like Medgar Evers to integrate Mississippi's universities and colleges, Coleman was confident that at the end of his term "the separation of the races in Mississippi will be left intact and will still be in full force and effect in exactly the same manner and form as we know it today." Though his stance on segregation was unswerving and in keeping with such radical predecessors as James K. Vardaman and Theodore Bilbo, Coleman was no rabble-rouser. He anticipated that the state would be buffeted by provocation from outside the state, especially from the federal courts, and from within from the nascent civil rights movement, and he thought that to protect Mississippi's "way of life" in the face of such agitation, "cool heads and calm judg-ment" must prevail, not "the amateur or the hothead." The new gover-nor's comment underestimated a defiant mood in the state that was prepared to defend states' rights, with violence if necessary, against the "illegal encroachment" of the federal government.[3]

In its own act of defiance, the state legislature provided an arsenal of weapons to fend off any attempt by the federal government to force integration on Mississippi's schools. First, the lawmakers sent Coleman a bill within a month of his inauguration repealing the state's compul-sory education laws, providing for the state to renounce its author-ity and responsibility to educate Mississippi children if and when the federal government forced the state to do so under conditions of racial integration. In other words, if forced to integrate, the state would close all public schools and make education a private matter. One does not know if the threat to close public schools was a serious option or political posturing. Certainly to those primarily concerned about economic development, the abolition of public schools would be a disaster, a move that would further isolate Mississippi as an economic backwater. Second, the legislature passed an interposition resolution whereby the lawmakers vowed to place the state government between the "encroaching" federal government and the right of Mississippians to enjoy states' rights in protection of "racial integrity." The interposition doctrine dated back to the early days of the republic when Thomas Jefferson and James Madison had claimed that a state had the right to stand between its citizens and harmful measures emanating from the federal government. Jefferson and Madison were referring specifically to the Alien and Sedition Acts of 1798, which the Federalists, centered in New England, had designed in order to curb the power of the Democratic-Republicans, centered in the southern states. Mississippi legislators saw a parallel between Jefferson's and Madison's defense of states' rights and their own. Lieutenant Governor Carroll Gartin made the case: "We are not willing to sit idly by and see rights reserved unto us trampled under foot and taken away by the Supreme Court. By all honorable and legal means, we are going to wage a great fight to keep our traditions." Third, the legislature created the Mississippi State Sovereignty Commission as part of the executive branch of state government. The official duties of the commission were spelled out in Section 5 of the bill:

> It shall be the duty of the commission to do and perform any and all acts and things deemed necessary and proper to protect the sovereignty of the State of Mississippi, and her sister states, from encroachment thereon by the Federal Government…and to resist the usurpation of the rights and powers reserved to this state and our sister states by the Federal Government or any branch, department, or agency thereof.[4]

While the carefully crafted bill never mentioned the terms segregation or integration, the commission's subsequent actions made clear that the new entity was in fact Mississippi's "segregation watchdog agency." Words like "encroachment" begged the question: Encroachment against what? The answer was racial integration. The commission was created to maintain segregation by ferreting out and neutralizing all attempts to advocate integration, whether by the hated NAACP or, to a lesser degree, by the few moderate whites in the state who, having hardly any traction at all in segregated Mississippi, resigned themselves to the inevitability of integration.

The central reality of the Sovereignty Commission is that it embodied Mississippi as a virtual police state in this era of racial turmoil. Its purpose can best be understood in its actions, such as its efforts to thwart Clyde Kennard's attempt to integrate Mississippi Southern College. As soon as Coleman and the Commission learned of Kennard's intention to apply, Coleman instructed Zack Van Landingham to compile a dossier on Kennard that might be useful in stopping his application. When completed, it was filed under the heading, "Race Agitators." Van Landingham's 37-page file contained nothing to indicate that Kennard was anything other than an "educated, intelligent, and courteous" man. He found nothing to impugn Kennard's character or anything to suggest that he was a civil rights "crusader." Nonetheless, Kennard was black, and that was sufficient grounds to dissuade him from registering.

Governor Coleman thought economic pressure might be effective in persuading Kennard to desist. He contacted the State Banking Board and asked them to send a bank examiner to Citizens Bank in Hattiesburg "for the purpose of examining the account of Clyde Kennard." Coleman wanted to see if the NAACP was funneling money into Kennard's account (they were not). Attorney General Joe Patterson concurred with the tactic, but the bank president declined to display Kennard's records on the grounds of confidentiality. The matter was dropped when Kennard withdrew his application for admission to Mississippi Southern.

While there is no evidence that the Commission was directly involved in framing Kennard for felonies, without question the governor and the Commission created a climate whereby others in Forrest County thought it permissible to stop at nothing to discredit Kennard. On two occasions Kennard faced criminal charges. The first came when he was in Mississippi Southern College President William D. McCain's office, where, after failing in one last attempt to dissuade him from continuing his application, McCain informed Kennard that his application was being rejected because of its "deficiencies and irregularities." Then, when Kennard reached his car in order to leave the campus, he was arrested by Forrest County Constable Lee Daniels for speeding, reckless driving, and possession of whiskey. Van Landingham and his associates seemed genuinely surprised at the arrest and swore they knew nothing about the matter and that it was the action of an overzealous local official. Justice of the Peace T. C. Hobby later found Kennard guilty of all charges. The final blow came when Kennard was framed in the chicken-feed case, found guilty, and sentenced to seven years at Parchman. Again, there is no direct evidence tying the Sovereignty Commission to that case, but without question the Commission contributed to the solution, which in fact was what Council leader Conner had earlier promised: to "take care" of Kennard and make sure that he left Hattiesburg and never returned.[5]

The *Brown* decision also spawned nongovernment organizations dedicated to preserving segregation, most notably the Citizens' Council. The group of planters, bankers, lawyers, and businessmen who organized the first Council in the Delta town of Indianola, Mississippi, was primarily concerned about withstanding attempts to integrate the state's schools. The threat was real. The NAACP led drives in at least five Mississippi school districts petitioning school boards to integrate schools in Jackson, Natchez, Vicksburg, Yazoo City, and Clarksdale. In each case, the local chapter of the Council organized campaigns to turn aside the attempts. In Jackson, Council President Ellis Wright met with school board members and the mayor and charged that the NAACP's ultimate goal was not school desegregation, but racial intermarriage. But, he warned, "If the NAACP thinks that we have the slightest idea of surrendering our Southland to a mulatto race...the NAACP had better think again." Assisted by pro-Council coverage in the Jackson *Daily News* and the *State Times*, Wright encouraged citizens to get in touch with the Council for means of defeating the petition. The "means" implied were those that had successfully stopped the petition in Yazoo City. There the Council took out a full-page ad in the local newspaper, the *Herald*, listed the names of all who had signed the desegregation petition, and asked readers to "look [the signers] over carefully." As a result, many of the petitioners lost their jobs, were refused credit at local banks and stores, and were unable to purchase necessary supplies. Within two months all but 6 of the original 53 signers asked to have their names removed from the petition, and the drive failed.

The people of Clarksdale were hesitant about organizing a Council. They were wary of a vigilante organization operating in their town. At the same time, they did not want to see their schools integrated. Council leader William J. Simmons recounted what happened in Clarksdale:

The good folks there had said, "We don't need a Citizens' Council, our niggers are good niggers, they don't want to integrate; if we organize a Citizens' Council it'll agitate them." But one bright morning they woke up with a school petition with 303 signers, including most of their "good ones." So they organized a Council. It's got 3,000 members now. The petition collapsed. They all started taking their names off. Really, about all the white people have to do is let 'em know they don't want to have all this stuff and that's about the end of it. Most of them got fired, I suppose.[6]

The Citizens' Council's tactics worked in all five cities. Faced with economic sanctions, blacks dropped their efforts to petition school boards for integration. Similar Council attacks thwarted voter registration drives. In the mid-1950s, the state had almost a half million blacks of voting age, but in 1954 only a little more than 20,000 voted, and in the next year the number fell to about 8,000. Although the U.S. Supreme Court had ruled the white primary unconstitutional, Mississippi Democrats challenged blacks who tried to vote. The chairman of the State Democratic Committee argued that "Negroes might be national Democrats but they are not Mississippi Democrats." He concluded, "We don't intend to have Negroes voting in this primary, but we also intend to handle it in a sensible, orderly manner." That "sensible, orderly manner" was similar to the effort to stop school integration: publicize the names of those who registered to vote and encourage white employers, creditors, and retailers to threaten their livelihoods.[7]

The Sovereignty Commission and the Citizens' Council could count on Mississippi's culture to reinforce their aims. In particular, most white churches were faithful allies in the fight to preserve racial segregation. After the desegregation order of 1954, most Mississippi churches defended the status quo and taught that segregation was part of the divine plan. To be sure, there were important exceptions. The Mississippi Diocese of the Episcopal Church made a general call for support of the Supreme Court's decision and for eventual integration in the state. A handful of other ministers and ministerial associations also made courageous calls for the extension of civil rights to all Mississippi citizens and pleaded for racial harmony and social justice. But the vast majority of messages from Mississippi pulpits echoed sentiments from the pews and denounced integration as federal government interference and the work of "outside agitators." When the Freedom

Riders arrived in Mississippi in the summer of 1961 to integrate such public facilities as bus stations, many white churches posted deacons and elders on their church steps to keep blacks and their supporters from disrupting services. The presumption was that if blacks really wanted to worship, they would go to "their" churches, and the very fact that they wanted to attend a white church meant that their motives were suspect.

Like churches, schools conditioned white Mississippians to accept uncritically white supremacy and states' rights. Students attended schools that were separate and unequal. Although Mississippi's public school teachers' salaries in the 1960s ranked lowest in the nation, the greatest cause of mediocre education in all-white schools came, not from dedicated teachers, but from near-constant concerns about the instruction in history and the social sciences voiced by the Citizens' Council, the American Legion, and the Daughters of the American Revolution. A case in point was the Council's insistence on forbidding the showing of the *The High Wall* in public schools. Donated by the Anti-Defamation League in the early 1950s, the 30-minute film depicted life inside the Warsaw ghetto. For six years the film had been shown in Mississippi schools without evoking comment or incident until the White Citizens' Council objected to it in 1959. The Council interpreted the film as teaching "children to pity their prejudiced parents who did not enjoy the enriching experience of intermingling with persons of different racial, ethnic and cultural backgrounds." The Council was particularly scandalized by a scene at the end showing "Americans and Poles walk[ing] arm-in-arm into the setting sun." The Council called the Anti-Defamation League "one of the most aggressive and highly financed pressure groups for integration in this country." In a private showing to members of the state legislature, one "alert" state senator agreed that *The High Wall* was "unfit for showing to Mississippi school children," and it was ordered removed. Educators protested the decision. The state audio-visual director noted that "this meaning has never been read into it," and state Superintendent of Education J. M. Tubb found "nothing objectionable about it."[8] But, politics trumped education, and Mississippi students retreated behind the walls of state-defined prejudice.

The arrival of the Freedom Riders also led to shrill oratorical outbursts against public instruction by Mississippi patriotic groups, particularly the Daughters of the American Revolution. Using the book *Brainwashing in the Schools* by Earlham College English professor E. Merrill Root as its bible, the DAR went on a campaign to purge about 40 books from the public school's adopted lists. A New England Quaker, Root was no segregationist, but his rabid anti-Communism served the interests of the DAR and state legislature just fine. While the book was widely ridiculed in the North, it was lauded in the South, particularly in Mississippi, for pointing out the subversive "liberal" texts that distorted American and state history. Among his more outlandish assertions, Root identified Thomas Jefferson with the John Birch Society and linked fluoridation with Communism and book-burning with Americanism. Both the DAR and the state legislature hired Root to help them identify and remove objectionable books from Mississippi schools. The governor applauded the efforts of Root and the DAR in cleaning up the book lists "so that children can be truly informed of the southern way of life." The Jackson *Daily News* joined the crusade, pointing out that adopted history textbooks were too liberal. Among other things, they failed to explain how labor unions coerced management, and they failed to relate how the "Negro people have done much to develop themselves" without the aid of federal government intervention. More level heads prevailed and stopped the book purging. They insisted that textbooks should be selected by teachers and not politicians, and many citizens, including legislators, found the adopted texts to be unobjectionable. When the wholesale book burning failed to materialize, one disappointed DAR member wailed that "Patriotic Americans seem to have no voice."[9]

After *Brown v. Board of Education*, the Citizens' Council advocated a systematic indoctrination of Mississippi children from their earliest days in school. The Council thought that by the fifth grade, students should receive lessons in states' rights, especially how the doctrine was a righteous justification for secession and the Civil War. Fifth- and sixth-grade lessons gave Mississippi's official version of events:

> Our forefathers were willing to stand up to the enemy because their freedom meant very much to them. Our Constitution is a contract. The states gave the federal government in Washington, D.C. some powers. But they kept most of the power for themselves. No other part of the United States is more American than the South. America was built by white men.[10]

The Citizens' Council hailed the success of the instruction manual. It reported that public reaction had been "keen and widespread" and that teachers were requesting "bundles" of the Council's monthly newspaper to use for discussing "current events" in the classroom. While the manual no doubt found receptive readers in some quarters, evidence suggests that teachers more widely shunned the attempt to direct their instruction. Planned subsequent installments were canceled.[11]

The Council also sponsored an annual statewide essay contest to promote states' rights, patriotism, and "racial integrity." Students could write on one of four topics: "Why I Believe in Social Separation of the Races of Mankind"; "Subversion in Racial Unrest"; "Why the Preservation of States' Rights Is Important to Every American"; and "Why Separate Schools Should Be Maintained for the White and Negro Races." Categorized by gender, winners of the best "boy" and best "girl" essays were awarded $500 college scholarships, with lesser amounts going to the second-, third-, and fourth-place winners. In July 1960, the Council reported that more than 8,000 students from 163 secondary schools participated and that English teachers in some schools made participation mandatory. One first-place winner was a girl from Hattiesburg High School, who wrote that white southerners would never bow to the will of federal judges "however exalted their seats or black their robes and hearts." Rather, she added defiantly, "we intend to obey the laws of God and the ... Constitution. As long as we live, so long shall we be segregated." Her male counterpart from Morton High School tried to explain "why we fight and will continue to fight until we have succeeded in maintaining segregation, our way of life, or until the Communists, with the aid of our own Supreme Court, have caused us to crumble from within and to fall like Rome of old."[12]

An important aspect of the Citizens' Council's efforts to control education was to impede the flow of information into the state, information from "outside agitators" who spread dangerous notions of egalitarianism. They sought to erect a *cordon sanitaire*, or a paper curtain around the state to filter the national news. The Council charged that the national news was dominated by propagandists bent on portraying the South in "the sorriest light possible." Accordingly, in 1959 the Council publicized its blacklisted organizations, a list of 74 public and private groups and agencies identified as promoting "civil rights and anti-South" legislation. Included on the list were the Young

Women's Christian Association, the American Friends Service Committee, the Anti-Defamation League, the Benevolent and Protective Order of Elks, the Methodist Church, and the Episcopal Church. Ten United States government agencies made the list, among them the Department of the Air Force, the Department of Justice, the Treasury Department, and the Interstate Commerce Commission.[13]

The Council found ready allies among patriotic groups who wished to shield white Mississippi students from being infected with the egalitarian notions that were surfacing all across the nation in the late 1950s and early 1960s. Allied organizations included the American Legion, the Daughters of the American Revolution, and the United Daughters of the Confederacy. The Council hired Mrs. Sara McCorkle, past president of the Mississippi American Legion Auxiliary, to become director of the Council's youth activities division in January 1958. The tireless Mrs. McCorkle traveled all over the state warning high school PTAs, teachers, and students about the "dangers of integration." With the cooperation of the DAR and the other allies, she scrutinized instructional materials for their possible "brainwashing" potential. One of the items she found objectionable was "Playtime Farm," an educational toy with plastic figures used in some elementary schools. She explained that the family group in the set had a "dark-skinned father and a white mother. Quite obviously," she asserted, "it was a subtle effort to promote intermarriage."[14]

Although he was one of the Citizens' Council's severest critics, Hodding Carter III, editor of the *Delta Democrat-Times*, acknowledged that no other organization had done more to stiffen resolve on maintaining racial segregation and silencing opposition. Writing in 1961, he noted that while other southern states were moving toward at least "token desegregation," Mississippi remained in firm control of the "diehard white-supremacists." And while many in other southern states were "grudgingly" beginning to accept integration as inevitable, in Mississippi it was "virtually impossible to find any public manifestation of the fatalism many whites" expressed privately. Carter claimed that to a "high degree" support for continued segregation was vested in the Citizens' Council, an organization whose presence was felt in every corner of the state.

For Carter, the Council had made the defense of segregation respectable in the eyes of most white Mississippians. Unlike the Klan, the Council expressed its aims not in violent language, but in "carefully crafted statements of states' rights and constitutionalism." Its leadership did not come from pool halls, but from the country club. And its membership was drawn from the middle and upper classes, giving its meetings an air of respectability that one would find at civic clubs such as Rotary or Lions. Like the Klan who also wanted to give their proceedings the cloak of divine sanction, the Council began its meetings with a prayer, usually delivered by a local Baptist minister. Then the Council leader, or perhaps an elected official, delivered the day's message, which sounded a consistent theme: continued adherence to segregation and states' rights. Steady attacks were made against those who threatened the Mississippi way of life—in particular, the NAACP and "Negro troublemakers" and their allies, white liberals and moderates.

As a result of its conservative and respectable leadership, no act of racial violence was ever linked directly with the Council. Rather than use crude and blunt instruments of violence to attain its goals, the Council preferred more indirect, yet equally effective, means of maintaining the status quo. Economic pressure against dissenting whites and Negroes was the primary weapon in the Council's arsenal. A minister who defended two men labeled by the Citizens' Council as "integrationists" was dismissed from his pulpit by his church's governing body, and clergymen across the state got the message. Dissenting newspaper publishers faced boycotts organized by the Council and/or competition from a newly established rival newspaper in the community.

When blacks became bolder in mounting an effective civil rights movement after the Emmett Till murder, the Council stepped up its campaign to besmirch the movement as the work of dangerous outsiders with links to the Communist Party. In what Hodding Carter called cultural isolation by means of "the big lie," the Council sullied the reputations of moderates and liberals by using insults that harkened back to rhetoric borne of the Civil War. Dissenters were called "scalawags," "nigger lovers," "nest foulers," and "renegade whites." The new charge that emerged in the late 1950s was that of "Communist" or "Communist sympathizer." Thus the Council linked the old rhetoric of the Civil War era with the new rhetoric of the McCarthy era to brand people as traitors to the South and to America. Aided by the Sovereignty

Commission, which brought in "professional anti-communist speakers and hunters," the Council was able to brand individuals and make the labels stick. For example, Professor James Silver, an Ole Miss history professor who was outspoken in calling for state compliance with the *Brown v. Board of Education* decision, was seldom referred to in the Jackson *Clarion-Ledger* without some allusion to his alleged Communist ties.

The Council's effectiveness lay not in staging spectacular acts, but in creating a climate of fear and intimidation. Until the Freedom Rides of 1961 and James Meredith's case against Ole Miss of the same year, the Council had effectively silenced opposition to segregation. Hodding Carter called the opposition that did exist "belated, isolated and ineffective." White Mississippians fell into three groups. Perhaps a majority accepted segregation and white supremacy as unquestioned fact and believed that race relations were matters for the state alone to handle. The federal government and all other "outsiders" had no role to play. Though they held these views with strong conviction, these were law-abiding citizens who opposed violence, whether perpetrated by the Klan or by the state. It should be noted, however, that while these individuals forswore violence personally, they adopted a somewhat detached perspective when *others* engaged in acts of violence against blacks. In other words, by remaining silent in the face of violence, these persons were part of its perpetration. Another sizable group agreed that segregation had worked for generations, but that things had changed around the country and that Mississippi needed to adapt to fit the times. These moderates tended to discuss their ideas only with each other and were not prone to speak out publicly. A third group, a minority, consisted of those whose willingness to use violence in the defense of segregation and states' rights matched their belief that their views were sacred principles. The climate that the Citizens' Council helped create made this group believe that its most extreme actions were justified.

Not all white Mississippians went along with the Council, but the opposition was restricted to a handful of newspaper editors and academics. Hazel Brannon Smith, editor of the Lexington *Advertiser*, advocated a progressive approach to race relations, and the Council responded by starting a rival paper with a strict segregationist editorial policy. Smith appealed to the community in an editorial that blasted the Council's campaign of fear and intimidation against anyone who dared hold a position on race different from theirs:

> Today in much of Mississippi we live in an atmosphere of fear. It hangs like a dark cloud over us, dominating almost every facet of public and private life.... No one speaks freely any more for fear of being misunderstood.... Almost every man and woman is afraid to try to do anything to promote good will and harmony between the races—afraid he or she will be taken for a mixer or worse.[15]

Ole Miss history professor James Silver agreed with Smith and won the enmity of the Council with his outspoken criticism of the Council and the climate it created. Without organized and effective opposition throughout the 1950s, Silver asserted, the Council created a "hyperorthodox social order" where dissenters remained silent or spoke into a gale of hate that drowned out moderate voices. He claimed that the "totalitarian society of Mississippi imposes on all its people an obedience to an official orthodoxy almost identical with the pro-slavery philosophy." Just as a majority of Mississippians in the antebellum period owned no slaves but supported the right to own slaves, so a majority in the 1950s went along with the Council's defense of segregation. To Silver, Mississippi had become a "Closed Society."[16] But, to members of the Citizens' Council he had become a pariah, and some members pressured Ole Miss officials to "get rid" of the outspoken professor "to stifle his degrading activities."[17]

Leading politicians in the state were outspoken in their support of the Council and in some cases, most notably that of Ross Barnett, were proud members. On March 7, 1960, Ross Barnett addressed a Citizens' Council convention in New Orleans and delivered a fiery talk entitled "Strength Through Unity." He prefaced his remarks by noting with pride that the Citizens' Council was born in Mississippi and that he was a member. "Friends," he intoned, "I am proud that I have been a CC member since the Councils' early days. I hope that EVERY SINGLE WHITE SOUTHERNER will join with me in becoming a member of this fine organization. The Citizens' Councils are fighting your fight—they deserve YOUR support!" He called the fight to preserve segregation a moral battle and linked the tradition of southern race relations to the region's strong religious heritage. He pointed out that "The South has a great spiritual heritage—it is the stronghold of religion in America—and our moral and spiritual leaders should provide us with the kind of leadership we will need so badly if our cause is to prevail." He closed by warning the Democratic Party that it took the South's 128 electoral votes for granted at its own peril. Barnett said, "I am a MISSISSIPPI DEMOCRAT—and the first word of that phrase means far more to me than the second!" He reminded the audience that in 1948, the South bolted when Truman turned the "wrong" way on race relations and that the South must be prepared once again to defy a Democratic Party that promotes integration.[18]

While the Council and the politicians who supported it filled the airwaves and newspapers with their defiant message, the Ku Klux Klan sounded a more ominous note in their clandestine meetings in woods and fields and in their acts of violence against blacks who sought to exercise their rights. Robert Shelton, Imperial Wizard of the Klan, made clear that the KKK was opposed not to Negroes, but to Negro organizations that were "sowing the seeds of discontent and racial hatred among the negroes of this country by preaching and teaching racial equality and mongrelization of the races." Whites enjoyed their right to rule and to define race relations because the land was theirs by right of inheritance, he claimed. Thus, blacks could live in peace only if they stayed in their place and lived within "their own institutions and within their own race without encroachment upon the rights of other races." Shelton pointed out that the Klan was faithful to the teachings of Christ. Indeed, he noted, at every meeting "Jesus Christ is lauded and his teachings expounded." Because of its Christian character, the Klan thought it unjust, Shelton declared, for Jews to belong.[19]

So when James Meredith returned to Mississippi in August 1960, he found little sign of any progress in race relations. He had hoped that the state had taken some steps toward accepting the *Brown* mandate to integrate public facilities, but he soon discovered that things had actually gotten worse. As he drove toward the Mississippi border, he stopped at a service station in Memphis that he had known from past experience to have integrated rest rooms. But this time, his wife encountered a sign that read, "White Ladies ONLY," and they were forced to go around back where they found "one cubbyhole for all Negroes to use—men and women and children. It was filthy, nasty, and stinking. The toilet wouldn't flush and there was no toilet paper or water to wash one's hands." That experience was the first of many over the next several days and weeks that convinced him that while "separate but equal" was no longer the law of the land, enforcement of the law of the land remained in Mississippi "at the discretion of the White Supremacists."[20]

What Meredith did not see as he drove down U.S. Highway 51 toward his hometown of Kosciusko was a civil rights movement that was expanding and bubbling up across the state. He was aware of the old warriors in the struggle, mainly male veterans like him who worked primarily through the NAACP. More and more young people from inside and outside the state, young women as well as young men, were demanding rights in bold tactics that confronted segregation and its enforcers on the streets. Indeed, about the time Meredith applied to Ole Miss in late 1960, black students from Tougaloo College outside Jackson staged the state's first sit-in at the Jackson Public Library. Police arrested and jailed the young men and women who defied the library's segregation policy by sitting in the white section. Undeterred, leaders of the Civil Rights Movement mounted a black voter registration drive in McComb. This time, more than a hundred Mississippi black students were joined by blacks and whites from northern states who marched to City Hall to register to vote. When white officials descended upon them to turn them aside, the students knelt and started to pray in nonviolent protest. Following the initial foray at McComb, staff members of the Student Nonviolent Coordinating Committee (SNCC) began setting up schools across the state instructing blacks on how to fill out the 21-question registration application and how to interpret the 285 sections of the Mississippi Constitution.[21]

James Meredith did not join the student movement in Mississippi. Indeed, he was critical of the civil rights movement, thinking that it only gnawed at the edges of institutionalized segregation rather than attacking it at its center. He was convinced that only economic equality would ever make black people equal and that the key to economic equality was equal educational opportunities. His personality also led him to embark on an individual quest to break down the racial barrier at Ole Miss. He was a loner, a quiet, almost mystical man who saw himself as tapped by destiny for this role. Charles Evers said that he and Medgar thought that Meredith was hardly the ideal test case at Ole Miss. "Meredith had guts," Charles wrote, "but he was a strange, mystical dude." Nonetheless, on January 29, 1961,

Mississippi State Sovereignty Commission's file photograph of James Meredith.
Originating Agency: Mississippi State Sovereignty Commission / Mississippi Department of Archives and History

Meredith told Medgar about his plans to enter Ole Miss, and Evers advised him to contact Thurgood Marshall of the NAACP's Legal Defense Fund for assistance. Evers was the first person outside Meredith's family to hear James' plans and could tell that the 29-year-old veteran was determined to see his plan through. He had spent nine years in an integrated society, and he was determined to integrate Mississippi in a quick, bold move that struck at the most sacred symbol of Mississippi's white supremacy. What neither knew, but both no doubt suspected, is that the Sovereignty Commission would soon mobilize to thwart Meredith's plans. Indeed, just as it had instructed Zack Van Landingham to undermine Clyde Kennard's admission attempt in Hattiesburg, within months after Meredith applied to Ole Miss the Commission dispatched investigators Andy Hopkins and Virgil Downey to Attala County to "obtain all information on James H. Meredith" and his parents.[22]

....

PART TWO

Confrontation at Ole Miss

CHAPTER 5

....

James Meredith Puts
Ole Miss on Trial

....

*...a carefully calculated campaign of delay, harassment, and
masterful inactivity"*
Judge John Minor Wisdom, U.S. Court of Appeals
for the Fifth District—1962

....

On June 25, 1962, James Meredith got a major break in his lawsuit against Ole Miss. The U.S. Court of Appeals for the Fifth
District in New Orleans found that he had been rejected by the
university solely because of race, thereby overturning the lower court's
decision. Four months earlier, Federal District Court Judge Sidney
C. Mize, a graduate of the University of Mississippi Law School and
a staunch segregationist, had found that Meredith had failed to prove
that Ole Miss had a policy of denying admission to Negro applicants.
Now the appellate court reversed Mize's decision. Writing the opinion
for the three-judge panel, Judge John Minor Wisdom wrote that "a full
review of the record leads inescapably to the conclusion that from the
moment the defendants discovered that Meredith was a Negro they
engaged in a carefully calculated campaign of delay, harassment, and
masterful inactivity...a defense designed to discourage and defeat by
evasive tactics." The court ordered the university to admit Meredith
and to take all measures to accelerate his admission.

Judge Wisdom's opinion exposed the state's legal challenges to
Meredith's application. From the moment he and the NAACP took

the case to court on May 31, 1961, the state had mounted a no-holds-barred defense, arguing that Meredith was rejected on nonracial grounds. To make their case, the state's lawyers offered a laundry list of reasons. First, they claimed that he was not a Mississippi resident, that he had not reestablished residency since returning to the state from his service in the Air Force. Second, they pointed out that his application was not accompanied by five letters of recommendation from Ole Miss alumni, letters required of all applicants. Third, they said he was unworthy of admission because he had registered to vote in a county where he was not a resident and that he was therefore a felon. (Meredith was from Attala County but had tried to register in Hinds County, where he was enrolled at Jackson State University, an all-black school.) Fourth, they maintained that his Jackson State credits were nontransferable because Jackson State was an unaccredited institution. Fifth, they suggested that Meredith was tied to the NAACP and was a mere tool of that organization and its agenda rather than a serious, qualified student interested in obtaining an education. And, sixth, they attacked his character. At one point, one of the defense attorneys, Dugas Shands, even suggested in court that Meredith had stolen the Smith Corona typewriter that he had used to type his letters to Ole Miss.

After the Court of Appeals ordered the state to admit Meredith forthwith, Governor Ross Barnett remained defiant, repeating his oft-quoted vow that no black would ever enter Ole Miss while he was governor. Elected governor in 1959, Barnett was a lifelong segregationist, and he was determined to keep the races separate in Mississippi even though segregation was falling in southern states all around. A Southern Baptist who taught Sunday school, his views on race were rooted in his religious convictions. "I believe that the Good Lord was the original segregationist," he declared on one occasion. On another he said, "The Negro is different because God made him different. His forehead slants back. His nose is different. His lips are different. And his color is sure different." His biggest fear, he added, was mixing the races because that would "lead inevitably to the production of an inferior mongrel." Besides, "God intended that we shouldn't mix."[1]

Meredith, although delighted with Judge Wisdom's decision, recognized that the battle for admission was far from over. He knew that his success depended on more than a court order. From the moment he filed for admission back in January 1961, he understood that the university and state would not voluntarily admit a black student and that they would have to be forced to admit a black to Ole Miss. The only way he could succeed, he thought, was to gain the full support of the federal government, including, if necessary, federal troops to protect him in Oxford just as Eisenhower sent them to Little Rock in 1957. Now that Governor Barnett had defied a federal court order, whether or not Meredith attended Ole Miss depended on the backing of President John F. Kennedy.

. . . . . .

The college experience for millions of American students begins with the ritual of identifying schools that fit their interests and applying for admission. When he applied in late January 1961, James Meredith had narrowed his choices to two colleges, with one being his clear preference and the other his backup. As a Mississippian he wanted to attend Ole Miss, the University of Mississippi. His reasons were clear and compelling: he wished to live in the state and make a difference as a professional and maybe as a politician. There was no better ticket than an Ole Miss degree for entrance into the state's power elite. Governor Barnett was an Ole Miss graduate, as were most of Mississippi's elected officials. They had been undergraduates or had attended the Ole Miss Law School or both, and Meredith wanted the opportunities within the state that an Ole Miss degree afforded. His backup was Atlanta University, admission to which he believed was a sure thing.

What made Meredith's application experience different from that of all others who sought admission to Ole Miss in 1961 was the fact that he was black. The university was, and had been from its 1848 inception, an all-white school. Further, the Mississippi's white establishment, despite the *Brown* decision, subscribed to the 1898 Supreme Court doctrine of separate but equal schools and accordingly maintained two state university systems divided along race lines. When Meredith applied to Ole Miss in 1961, he was currently a political science major at Jackson State, but he had come to realize that the education he was receiving there was inferior to what he could expect at Ole Miss, and he knew that a JSU degree did not carry the cachet of a diploma from Ole Miss. Meredith had another goal; he wanted to desegregate the University of Mississippi, not just to gain economic and professional opportunity for himself, but for all black Mississippians as well.

James Meredith knew that his assault against white supremacy was aimed at the stronghold of segregation. He had been stationed at Topeka, Kansas, when the *Brown* case was handed down. A white lieutenant colonel from the Mississippi Delta, who knew of James' anti-segregation sentiments, befriended him and even sympathized with his views on desegregation but warned Meredith that white Mississippians would never give up their segregated society, adding that they would kill every black, if necessary, to preserve the system of white supremacy. Civil rights leaders also viewed Mississippi as the toughest state to crack. Roy Wilkins, Executive Secretary of the NAACP, called Mississippi "the snarling dog state" and called on "all decent Americans" to target Mississippi "in an effort to erase the disgrace this state has brought upon our country in the eyes of all humanity." Martin Luther King declared that Mississippi "historically had the worst record on racial violence, education, infant mortality, and living standards for its black residents." He deemed tactics employed elsewhere in the South "impractical or even suicidal" in Mississippi.[2] Meredith regarded Mississippi as the "forbidden territory—the epitome of white domination." He noted that the "Mississippi system of White Supremacy had gone virtually unchallenged since it was established following the Civil War."[3]

Meredith knew well the challenge he faced and understood that if he confronted the white establishment on its terms, he would lose, just as Evers, King, and Kennard had before him. So he developed a threefold strategy that would enable him to maintain the offensive while putting the state on the defensive. The first, and most important, part of his plan was to force the federal government to support his admission, with troops if necessary. The only way he could succeed, Meredith believed, was to have greater force on his side than Barnett could muster on the other. Second, he determined that to ensure that no one—white or black—could dissuade him from his goal; he must make himself utterly unapproachable. Only by going it alone could he make certain that he did not become a pawn for Mississippi civil rights leaders who might urge him to compromise or use him for their own ends. He expressed his wariness of state civil rights leaders in an interview: "I distrusted the Mississippi NAACP. They were too willing to settle for less than full rights." He did, however, admire the legal skills of the national NAACP and welcomed their assistance in the court battle that he knew would be necessary. Third, he insisted that he conduct his battle in public, under the bright light of publicity. That, he thought, gave him protection. While whites terrorized in secrecy, he determined that he could put fear in white political leaders by having their every act scrutinized publicly in the probing scrutiny of the national media.[4]

On January 21, 1961, Meredith wrote Registrar Robert Ellis requesting an application for admission. Meredith knew that it was late for seeking admissions for the spring semester, but he wanted to initiate the process in hopes of beginning classes in the summer session if not before. The date has added significance for Meredith's strategy to desegregate Ole Miss. It was the day after John Kennedy's inauguration as president. Kennedy's election inspired Meredith to proceed with his plan, hopeful that the young president would make good on his campaign promise to protect the civil rights of all Americans.

Meredith received a prompt reply from the registrar. To any expectant applicant, the letter was encouraging. "We are pleased to know of your interest in becoming a member of our student body," it began, in the same polite response that all applicants received. It continued, "If we can be of further help to you in making your enrollment plans, please let us know."[5] There was no mention of the lateness of the application for the upcoming semester.

Thus, in the initial exchange between Meredith and Ole Miss, there was nothing out of the ordinary; indeed it was the same cordial and informative tone that thousands of applicants had encountered in their quests for admission. That changed, however, in the next round of correspondence. Meredith completed the application and returned it to Registrar Ellis with a brief and momentous note: "I sincerely hope that your attitude toward me...will not change upon learning that I am not a white applicant. I am an American-Mississippi-Negro citizen." He also explained that in lieu of the required five letters of recommendation from Ole Miss alumni, he had enclosed five letters from Negro citizens of his community. He added that he had requested that transcripts from the previous universities that he had attended be sent to the registrar.[6]

Meredith understood that his application was unlikely to breeze through the review process like those of qualified white students. Prior to making application, he had discussed his intentions with Medgar

Evers, the field secretary for the NAACP in Mississippi. In 1954, Evers had applied for admission to Ole Miss but had been rejected. He told Meredith that the university's registrar had employed all sorts of delaying actions to discourage him from pursuing enrollment and then, when Evers persisted for nine months, turned him down on a technicality. Evers' letters of recommendation from "prominent" citizens had come from residents of Newton County where Medgar grew up, not from Bolivar County where he resided at the time of his application. Meredith knew that the hurdle for blacks seeking admission was even higher in 1961 than it had been in 1954. After the Evers' attempt, the university changed its admissions procedure to require letters of recommendation from five alumni, which meant five letters from white people.

Upon Evers' advice, Meredith wrote Thurgood Marshall, Chief Counsel of the NAACP's Legal Defense and Educational Fund in New York. Marshall had represented the plaintiffs in the 1954 *Brown v. Board of Education* case. In his letter to Marshall, Meredith stated his conviction that his academic qualifications were "adequate," a claim similar to the one he made in his admission letter to the Ole Miss registrar. He explained that while he had been stationed in Japan, he had completed 34 semester hours of work in the University of Maryland's Overseas Program. His grades in those courses had been three A's and nine B's. In addition, he informed Marshall that he was currently enrolled at Jackson State, where in the fall quarter he had received one A, one B, and one C in work completed. In his mind, his academic record warranted admission to Ole Miss. But, in anticipation of being rejected on the basis of racial discrimination, he asked Marshall and the NAACP's Defense Fund to support his case through the court system if necessary.[7] Marshall was cautious and wrote Medgar Evers to learn more about Meredith. A school desegregation case in Mississippi would be challenging under the best of circumstances and would be impossible if the litigant was not a legitimate candidate for admission.

Meredith's relationship with the NAACP became an issue in the ensuing court case. The state asserted in court that he was "hand-picked" by the NAACP to challenge Mississippi's segregated school system, while Meredith insisted that he acted alone on his own initiative and gained NAACP support only after careful vetting. The evidence suggests that it was less of a conspiracy than the state made it out to be, yet there was some coordination between Meredith and the NAACP. Through his ties with the Legal Defense Fund, Meredith the individual was linked to the organizational activities within the broader civil rights movement.

When Meredith's application reached Robert Ellis, it was no longer just another request for admission. Now that the applicant was known to be a black student, a special set of procedures would be followed. As Medgar Evers' earlier application had indicated, the university had put in place new admissions requirements, but officials knew that after the *Brown* decision there would be more applications by black students. Therefore, any application from a black would be handled with care and would follow a process established just for such an eventuality. The goal was to deny admission in a way that would stand up in court cases that would surely follow. Thus Ellis sent Meredith's application to the Mississippi Board of Trustees for Institutions of Higher Learning. The maintenance of a strict color barrier at Ole Miss was not just a university concern, it was a state priority. On February 7, the Board of Trustees adopted two new admissions requirements aimed directly at Meredith. First, state universities could accept transfer students "only when the previous program of the transferring college is acceptable to the receiving institution." Second, no student would be allowed to transfer mid-term unless he or she was an "exceptional student."[8] Accordingly, in a telegram dated February 4, Registrar Ellis informed Meredith that his application had been received too late for consideration for the spring semester.

Recognizing that the university was beginning its strategy of indefinite postponement, Meredith on February 7 wrote the U.S. Department of Justice for assistance. It was his first attempt to enlist the federal government on his side in the upcoming battle. President Kennedy had campaigned on the promise to fight for equal rights, and Meredith now wanted him to act on that promise. He made two points in his letter: first, that he was a United States citizen, and second, that he expected the Justice Department to protect his rights as a citizen. He opened by expressing regret that he or any American had to "clamor with such procedures" in order to "gain just a small amount of his civil and human rights." He informed the Justice Department of the state's historic use of "delaying tactics" and declared his resolve to obtain an Ole Miss education as the first step toward equal professional opportunity in the state. He wrote, "a Negro born in Mississippi can write himself off of the potential list of all of the professions, except teaching and preaching." He closed by asking that the federal agencies "use their power...to insure the full rights of citizenship for our people."[9]

Throughout the spring semester, Meredith heard nothing further from the university about his application for admission to the summer session. Finally, he received a letter dated May 25 informing him that his application had been denied. The registrar gave two reasons for the rejection. First, the university recognized transfer credits only from member institutions of the Southern Association of Colleges and Secondary Schools (SACS), and because Jackson State was not a SACS institution, his credits were rejected. Of course, Meredith would later point out that Jackson State was a state university that state officials had long trumpeted as part of Mississippi's commitment to "separate but equal" schools. Second, Meredith's letters of recommendation were not from Ole Miss alumni and therefore did not comply with university guidelines.

Within a week of receiving the rejection letter, Meredith and the NAACP took the case to court, filing a civil rights discrimination complaint in the U.S. District Court, Southern District of Mississippi in Jackson. Though Meredith had been critical of the state civil rights movement, he benefited from recent initiatives. By the time he filed his suit, the face of Mississippi's civil rights movement had changed dramatically. Instead of being led by middle-aged black males in Mississippi closely tied to the NAACP and committed to seeking legal remedies, the movement was becoming more diversified. The movement accepted a growing number of younger members, including many college students, welcomed women as well as men, aligned with more youthful organizations such as the Congress of Racial Equality (CORE) and the Student Nonviolent Coordinating Committee (SNCC) while maintaining ties to the NAACP, welcomed the assistance of activists from outside the state, and employed the tactics of civil disobedience and politics-in-the-street in addition to courtroom maneuvering. CORE was founded by a group of students at the University of Chicago in 1942 for the purpose of fighting for equal rights for all citizens, including African Americans. In the summer of 1961, just as Meredith filed his suit, the organization launched its boldest drive: a caravan of buses carrying blacks and whites from Washington, D.C., to New Orleans for the purpose of desegregating public transportation facilities in the South, such as waiting rooms and rest rooms at bus stations. The Supreme Court had ordered the desegregation of public transportation, but the Deep South had defied the ruling. CORE's idea was to drive through the heart of the South on a route that went through Tennessee, Alabama, and Mississippi, en route to Louisiana, and, along the way, passengers of both races would demand equal access to waiting rooms, rest rooms, and lunch counters.

There was precedent for such a challenge. In 1944 a young black woman, Irene Morgan, who worked in a wartime aviation factory in Virginia, boarded a Greyhound Bus for her home in Baltimore. When she, like Rosa Parks later, refused to give up her seat in the back of the bus to a white couple, she was forcefully dragged from the bus by the sheriff of Middlesex County, Virginia. The NAACP took up her cause, and though her case did not end racial discrimination on public transportation, it did contribute to the growing fight among African

NAACP lawyers: Constance Baker Motley and Jack Greenberg.
© *Bettmann/Corbis*

Americans who insisted on ending segregation. The incident inspired a ditty that expressed the sentiments of the Freedom Riders of 1961:

> You don't have to ride jim crow,
> You don't have to ride jim crow,
> Get on the bus, sit any place,
> Cause Irene Morgan won her case,
> You don't have to ride jim crow.[10]

CORE Director James Farmer explained the goal of the group dubbed the Freedom Riders in 1961: "We felt we could count on the racists of the South to create a crisis so that the federal government would be compelled to enforce the law." The riders expected violence and were prepared to endure it for the cause of equal opportunity. Their expectations were realized in a flurry of violence from whites who slashed the tires of the buses and police officers who severely beat riders who entered segregated areas. At Nashville, some wanted to turn back, but Nashville SNCC students reenergized the Freedom Rides and took them deeper into the South. In Birmingham, Alabama, Police Commissioner Bull Connors refused to provide police protection to the riders who were then at the mercy of a mob that severely beat many of the protestors. Alabama Governor John Patterson, who was elected with the enthusiastic support of the KKK,[11] voiced the prevailing sentiment of whites across the Deep South: "When you go somewhere looking for trouble, you usually find it.... You just can't guarantee the safety of a fool and that's what these folks are, just fools." Though beaten and frightened, the riders elected to continue their journey into the soul of the segregated South—Mississippi, where their actions would intersect with that of James Meredith.

The Freedom Riders arrived at the Jackson bus station just a few months before Meredith began his quest for admission to Ole Miss. However, not only did Meredith not participate in the riders' protest, he was critical of it. He thought that the riders were approaching the fight for civil rights in a piecemeal fashion by attempting to gain access to public facilities. He believed that blacks should demand full civil rights, which could be done only by dismantling the state's power structure that propped up segregation. Nonetheless, the protests of the Freedom Riders in Jackson and their mass jailing brought national attention to the fight for civil rights in Mississippi, and that certainly dovetailed with his strategy of proceeding under the bright lights of publicity. Moreover, the Freedom Riders confronted the Kennedy Administration with a thorny civil rights problem much as Meredith had confronted the Barnett Administration with the pressing problem of school desegregation. While President Kennedy would like to have ignored the mounting civil rights struggle in the South, he was under increasing pressure to make his administration an active partner with those fighting for their constitutional rights. The presence of the Freedom Riders also fostered a siege mentality among white Mississippians, who became more determined than ever to defend the status quo. So as the Jackson police arrested scores of protestors and took them to crowded jails, both the nation and the state watched to see what the respective responses would be from federal and state officials. The dramatic events had succeeded in forcing the Kennedy administration to protect them and all who were fighting for racial justice in the South. So in the summer of 1961, Meredith, representing the "old" civil rights movement, and the Freedom Riders, representing the "new," in their different ways assaulted the barricades of Mississippi segregation.

Meredith was represented in Judge Mize's court by a veteran of the civil rights movement. Constance Baker had written the original complaint in the *Brown* case and was well aware of legal defenses that segregationists mounted against any encroachment. The complaint that she filed on Meredith's behalf specified that the requirement of alumni recommendations was unconstitutional because it placed a special burden on black students because all alumni were white. The complaint also stated that Mississippi, in violation of federal law, required that "Negroes and whites [be] educated in separate institutions of higher learning." The case asked for a "speedy hearing" in order for Meredith to enter Ole Miss for the summer session, but it also made clear that this was a class action suit aimed at preventing discrimination against any black applicant to any of Mississippi's white institutions.

The suit filed by the NAACP on his behalf charged the university with pursuing a general policy of segregation and that the registrar had denied admission solely on the basis of race. But Judge Sidney Mize was unsympathetic. A 74-year-old judge who had been on the federal bench since 1937, Mize found more convincing the arguments of Ole Miss's lawyers that the registrar had followed procedures that applied to all applicants, regardless of color. After the lawyers rested, Judge Mize refused to hear arguments on Meredith's charges until he had established that Meredith was indeed a resident. For more than six months Mize deliberated, thus preventing Meredith from enrolling in summer school and then from entering in the fall of 1961 and the spring of 1962.

Finally, Meredith got his date in court when Mize set a trial date for January 24, 1962. However, the outcome was hardly what he had hoped; Mize ruled that Meredith had failed to prove that the university had a policy denying admission to Negro applicants. Further, he asserted that before the *Brown* case Mississippi had practiced racial segregation, but afterwards the state had changed its policy and now no practice or policy prevented a "qualified" Negro from entering Ole Miss. The NAACP immediately appealed the decision to the U.S. Court of Appeals for the Fifth District in New Orleans.

When Judge John Minor Wisdom handed down the decision overturning Mize's judgment, the matter was not over. Appellate Judge Ben Cameron, a member of the Fifth Circuit Court, but not one who sat on the Meredith case, entered a stay on Wisdom's order until the Supreme Court could rule on the case. A dedicated segregationist with a long record of upholding separation of the races, Cameron's action meant yet another delay for Meredith. But, two weeks after Cameron's ruling, the Kennedy Administration for the first time took action on behalf of Meredith, thus vindicating his belief that John Kennedy's election would make a difference in his bid for admission to Ole Miss. The Justice Department submitted a memo to the Supreme Court asking Justice Hugo Black to set aside Cameron's stay. A week later, the Court instructed James McShane, Chief U.S. Marshal, to begin organizing a contingent of marshals for possible action in Mississippi. U.S. Marshals are the enforcement arm of the federal court system, and it fell to them to help enforce court orders. On September 10, Justice Black set aside Cameron's stay and ordered Meredith admitted to Ole Miss forthwith. Quickly following that order, Judge Mize issued an injunction against any and all attempts by the University to block or delay Meredith's admission.

Now attention shifted to Ross Barnett and the state of Mississippi. Would the governor comply with what was now the law of the land, or would he continue his defiant stance? Barnett's campaign for governor in 1959 had been a campaign of fear. In his speeches he castigated the federal government, a despised villain who was bent on violating Mississippi's sovereign right to preserve its segregated society. As he watched the Meredith case move forward, Barnett's message became increasingly shrill in the defense of states' rights and segregation. The U.S. Supreme Court had overturned the cherished doctrine of separate but equal schools. Republican President Dwight Eisenhower had sent troops into Little Rock to enforce a desegregation order. Now the liberal Democratic president, whose nomination Barnett had opposed at the Democratic National Convention in Los Angeles, raised the specter of throwing the power of the federal government behind Meredith's quest for admission to Ole Miss.

In seeking a legal doctrine to justify rejecting Meredith's application, Barnett looked to the pre-Civil War past for guidance. He placed his hope on the thoroughly discredited doctrine of interposition, the notion that a state can declare any federal law null and void within the bounds of the state if the law is repugnant to the state's interest. The reasoning was that the Tenth Amendment denied authority to the federal government over all matters not delegated to it by the states, and because education was not one of those delegated powers, it rested solely under state authority. The courts had repeatedly and recently declared interposition unconstitutional. One month before Meredith applied to Ole Miss, the U.S. Supreme Court in a Louisiana segregation case had declared, "The conclusion is clear that interposition is not a Constitutional doctrine. If taken seriously, it is an illegal defiance of Constitutional authority." As a lawyer, Barnett knew that interposition was bankrupt as a legal strategy; nevertheless, he invoked interposition in opposing Meredith's entrance to Ole Miss. He believed that he could succeed merely by calling Kennedy's bluff.

Whether or not the governor believed that interposition was sound legal strategy, he knew that it was shrewd politics in Mississippi. Therefore, he employed no-compromise rhetoric in speeches across the state, depicting the confrontation not as one between Barnett and Meredith, but as one between the "naked and arbitrary power" of the federal government and "the right of self-determination" for the sovereign state of Mississippi to conduct its affairs. Invoking images and language of 1861, he said, "We must either submit to the unlawful dictates of the Federal Government or stand up like men and tell them NEVER!" He added in a typical speech, "I have said in every county in Mississippi that no school in our state will be integrated while I am your Governor. I repeat to you tonight—NO SCHOOL WILL BE INTEGRATED IN MISSISSIPPI WHILE I AM YOUR GOVERNOR!"[12]

Barnett knew his audience. For Mississippians, race was not just an important political issue, it was the paramount issue. One reporter from outside the state found in his daily rounds that whites associated race with everything, no matter how mundane. As he traveled through the state in 1962, reporter Robert Massie visited white Mississippians of all socioeconomic backgrounds and of various cultural sensitivities and found that the one thing that they shared was a preoccupation with race. During one week in Jackson, he gathered the following sample of sentiments from a wide assortment of individuals:

+ A gracious lady in Jackson: "Listen, if I went to a dinner party and admitted that somewhere in the passage of immemorial time Mississippi might change its views on integration, we'd have a mighty unpleasant evening."

+ A cotton farmer in the Delta: "They tell us it would be the Christian thing for Negro children to go to school with white children. I honestly don't think it would be Christian to plunge those children together. Negroes are different. One third of their children are illegitimate. They won't even go to their own schools. You can send a school bus right to the door and they won't get on."

+ A judge: "The race question has made for more bad legislation and more bad court decisions in this state than you can possibly imagine."

+ A young couple watching a Negro entertainer on TV: *He:* 'See, the damn niggers are trying to take over the country.' *She:* 'Aw, leave it on. I want to watch.'

+ A small-town newspaper owner: "In this town, you're either black or white. We have two Chinese families here. Both own grocery stores. One has married with the blacks, the other is accepted by the whites. The two families don't speak to each other."

+ A community leader in the Delta: "I'm worried because so many cultured people have really begun to hate Negroes. My sister, for example, always enjoyed Negro people. Now she can't stand them. It's because the Negroes have changed. They want more. They don't want to stay in their place."[13]

Barnett also knew that in Mississippi politics contempt for the federal government was second only to race as an explosive issue for whites. Regarding the government's intervention in civil rights issues as a "Second Reconstruction," whites deemed any exercise of federal power in support of blacks' demands for full citizenship to be an unconstitutional assault on states' rights. The Kennedys, especially Robert, personified federal evil. State Senator Jimmie Christenberry expressed the depth of white Mississippian's feelings toward the Kennedys: "If the sun didn't come up tomorrow, people wouldn't really care. They'd just say, 'Sure is dark today. Damn Kennedys!'"[14]

Feeding off such sentiment, Barnett defied the federal court order to admit Meredith. On September 13 the governor went on statewide radio and television to proclaim in no uncertain terms: "We will not surrender to the evil and illegal forces of tyranny." Barnett invoked the doctrine of interposition: "In obedience to legislative and constitutional sanction I interpose the rights of the sovereign State of Mississippi to enforce its laws and to regulate its own internal affairs without interference on the part of the federal government or its offices." The governor knew that for his stance to succeed, there must be complete unity among all elected officials, and he soon received a resolution of support from the state legislature and a telegram of congratulations from the Mississippi congressional delegation in Washington. However, Barnett made one statement that caused considerable anxiety by many in Mississippi including Ole Miss students. He promised that schools in general and Ole Miss in particular "will not be closed if this can possibly be avoided—but they will not be integrated." Thirty years earlier another Mississippi governor, Theodore Bilbo, had fired more than a hundred professors at the state universities, and all of the schools lost their accreditation because of the governor's interference. Joining students and faculty who did not want to see the university closed, even if Meredith were admitted, were many moderates in the state, including businessmen who knew that economic development depended on a sound educational system. They considered any state action that jeopardized the university's accommodation to be reckless and irresponsible.

Barnett had another problem: how to defend states' rights and race segregation without plunging the university and state into violence. The first potential for violence on the campus presented itself on September 20, when Meredith made his initial attempt to register for classes. An ominous sign of what the day might bring appeared at 5:25 A.M., when a 14 foot by 27 foot cross made of cloth sacks was burned on the street between the men's dormitories. No one knew if students or outsiders were behind the incident; an eyewitness reported seeing a car speed away shortly after the cross ignited. Campus police were able to remove the debris without incident. But, beginning early in the day a crowd of from 50 to 200 students gathered in front of the Lyceum in anticipation of the looming confrontation between Meredith and Barnett. By mid-afternoon the crowd had swelled to around 2,000, with many nonstudents on the scene. At one point, a known local troublemaker attempted to haul down the American flag and replace it with the Confederate Stars and Bars, but a group of students led by student body president Gray Jackson raised the American flag again. Barnett arrived at the Oxford airport at 2:30 and, when asked if Meredith would become a student at Ole Miss, he shouted "Hell no!"[15]

Barnett was armed with full authority from various state agencies that had scrambled at the last minute to give the governor ammunition for denying Meredith admission. Earlier that day, a Hinds County justice of the peace tried Meredith in absentia on charges of false voter registration, found him guilty, and sentenced him to pay a fine of $100 plus serve one year in the county jail. The ruling meant in the parlance of Mississippi justice that Meredith had now been convicted of a crime of "moral turpitude." The conviction cleared the way for the Mississippi Legislature to pass Senate Bill No. 1501, which denied admission to any state school any person "who has a criminal charge of moral turpitude pending against him" or "has been convicted of any criminal offense and not pardoned." Aimed solely at Meredith, the measure contained a provision to exempt children of the legislators and their friends, notably one individual who was currently an undergraduate now facing difficulties in seeking admission to the law school because of charges of manslaughter committed while intoxicated. Thus, the law excluded "any charge or conviction of traffic law violations, violation of the state conservation laws and state game and fish laws, or manslaughter as a result of driving while intoxicated or under the influence of intoxicants." While the legislature armed Barnett with solid legislative authority to deny Meredith admission on "nonracial" grounds, the state's Board of Trustees for Higher Education empowered him to act as registrar in the case. The board wanted no part in defying a federal court order, so they stepped aside and allowed Barnett to handle the matter directly, and in doing so, to face contempt of court charges.

There was nothing ordinary about the admissions hearing that took place on the campus of the University of Mississippi on Thursday afternoon, September 20, 1962. First, it did not take place in the Registrar's Office housed in the Lyceum Building where matters concerning student admissions usually were held; rather it occurred in a nondescript structure, the University Continuation Center, located on the eastern fringe of the Ole Miss campus, far from the centrally situated Lyceum. Second, the timing of the meeting was noteworthy, coming late because classes for the fall semester were about to begin. Indeed, orientation for new students had been held the previous day, and now students were in the process of selecting courses and buying books in preparation for the first day of classes the following Monday. But, what most distinguished this particular admissions hearing was the cast of characters that faced each other in the meeting. The applicant was James Meredith, a Mississippian from Kosciusko, who was black, and Ole Miss had never admitted a black person since its first class convened in 1848. But, unlike blacks who earlier had sought admission, Meredith was not alone. By his side was James P. McShane, Chief U.S. Marshall, two deputy marshals, and Department of Justice attorney St. John Barrett. Facing Meredith was Governor Ross Barnett, who in this instance acted as university registrar even though Ole Miss Registrar Robert Ellis sat beside him. This was a showdown unlike any seen in Mississippi since Reconstruction. A black man, backed by the authority and power of the federal government, demanded his civil rights; a white man, backed by the authority and power of the State of Mississippi, claimed states' rights to deny Meredith his civil rights. The showdown represented far more than two individuals. His protests notwithstanding, James Meredith, supported by the state NAACP and the national NAACP Legal Defense Fund, was a part of the larger civil rights struggle. And, Barnett was an individual immersed in Mississippi's cultural climate of white supremacy, and, as an astute politician, he played off that culture's tendencies for his gain.

The meeting inside the Continuation building was brief and predictable. Meredith opened by saying to Registrar Robert Ellis, "I want to be admitted to the University." Informing Meredith that Governor Barnett was now the registrar, Ellis turned the meeting over to the governor who proceeded to read his interposition proclamation and denied Meredith admission. Barnett prevailed on that occasion, but he had reason to worry. On previous confrontations between whites and blacks in Mississippi, whites had a monopoly of power, but in this instance there was the possibility that the federal government would intervene on Meredith's behalf. Nonetheless, Barnett called Kennedy's bluff, betting that the president, seeking re-election in 1964, would not spend valuable political capital backing a black man in the heart of the segregated South. Barnett worried more that Mississippi whites were far from unified in their support of his stance. Just a week earlier, Ira Harkey of the *Pascagoula Chronicle* wrote a stinging editorial criticizing Barnett's defiance and the extreme views that it encouraged,

Meredith arrives on Ole Miss campus.
AP IMAGES/Associated Press

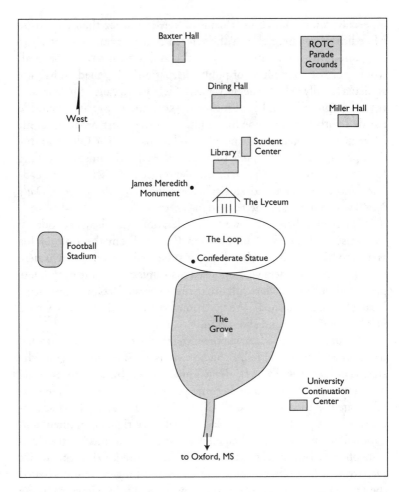

Map of the Ole Miss campus.

especially comments about closing Ole Miss rather than admitting Meredith. "Anywhere else in the United States," Harkey wrote, "the suggestion that a state university be closed down for any reason at all would not rise to the level of public discussion." He called on Mississippians to rally behind the university officials who called for calm and reason to prevail and, by all means, to keep the university open. He pleaded with the governor to comply with the court order to admit Meredith in the name of democracy and humanity. The Ole Miss student paper, the *Mississippian*, took a similar editorial position, calling for calm and reason to prevail, and denounced the "screaming headlines and sensationalized stories" streaming from the *Jackson Daily News*, which fueled Barnett's extreme rhetoric.[16]

On September 20, however, moderation was drowned out by extremists outside the Continuation Center. From the time of his arrival to his departure, Meredith was subjected to jeering townsmen, students, and outsiders who opposed his admission. Some bystanders predicted violence if Meredith broke the university's color barrier. One local white man warned, "We got some boys around here that would just love to come in and shoot him."[17]

No one could predict whether Meredith's efforts would succeed or whether they would fail, as had previous attempts to integrate the state's colleges. Would he be denied final success by last-minute legal maneuvering? Or, would he become yet another victim of state brutality such as that which befell Clyde Kennard? He did have advantages that his predecessors had lacked. The civil rights movement and national media attention helped level the field against entrenched state officials. But, success was by no means assured. While the Justice Department had offered some support when Judge Cameron issued the stay against the appellate court's order to admit Meredith, there was no assurance that the Kennedy Administration would back that court order with force if necessary. The outcome was uncertain, and James Meredith would need to muster all of the courage, determination, and perseverance that he had demonstrated in the previous 18 months in order to prevail in the next two weeks.

CHAPTER 6

The Battle of Ole Miss

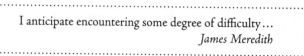

I anticipate encountering some degree of difficulty...
James Meredith

On Friday, September 28, 1962, the Ole Miss campus was a tranquil setting for a student body abuzz with excitement and anticipation. Situated on almost a thousand acres of rolling hills and dotted with hardwood groves, the picturesque campus in north Mississippi, dormant over the hot summer, was now alive with all the activities of a new academic year. Students had completed registration for the fall semester and were attending their first classes. Hundreds of pledges had joined fraternities and sororities during rush week, an annual ritual at Ole Miss with its rich Greek tradition. The nationally ranked football team had won its first game against Memphis State and was traveling to Jackson to play the University of Kentucky on Saturday. Indeed, about half of the roughly 4,500 students would make the 175-mile trip down to the state capital for a weekend of revelry and football.

Although the federal court order to admit James Meredith as the first black student at the university represented a cloud over the serene campus, there was reason for students to be optimistic about the ultimate outcome. First, Chancellor J. D. Williams provided the voice of calm and reason. Throughout the summer he had urged alumni groups to lend their "courageous support" in protecting the university's freedom. To him that meant that the university must investigate "*all* ideas, good and bad." With the Meredith case nearing its tortuous traversal through the court system, "all ideas" included that of integration. Many students agreed with Williams and thought it wise to adapt to the new reality rather than jeopardize the university's future by defying a court order. Second, most students saw Governor Barnett's defiant words and deeds as politics-as-usual in a state where every governor vowed to defend segregation. Even though a majority no doubt preferred the continuation of segregation, they did not wish to see the university turned into a battlefield over the issue. Third, as they prepared for the big weekend, their thoughts centered not on politics but on what mattered to college students everywhere when classes were over for the week: a bit of fun and relaxation.

For James Meredith, Friday was another day of frustration and anxious waiting in Memphis. On the previous day, he and his federal escorts had set out on yet another futile attempt—his third in a week—to register at the Ole Miss campus in Oxford, located 70 miles from Memphis. Central to Meredith's calculations all along had been the necessity of Washington's full, firm, and unstinting support. He was confident that in his impending final showdown with Barnett, he would prevail if the federal resolve held. But, he was beginning to worry about that resolve. He had heard rumors that President Kennedy and Governor Barnett were hatching a deal in his case. Later, he wrote, "I had no trust in either of them, and less trust for Kennedy than for Barnett, because the law barred Barnett from re-election, but I knew John Kennedy wanted to be re-elected."[1] At one point as the convoy left Memphis, Meredith told the federal officials to turn around, that he did not trust the government's sincerity in pledging adequate force to ensure his safe enrollment at Ole Miss. His escorts pleaded with him to reconsider, and he reluctantly consented to proceed.

Perhaps Meredith's worries stemmed from his fear that the Kennedys' support would falter as tensions mounted. In fact, transcripts of telephone conversations between the White House and the governor's mansion indicate that the Kennedys remained resolute in their determination to see that Meredith was peacefully admitted to

Ole Miss. In 20 telephone conversations between September 15 and September 28, the two sides worked out a secret plan for the peaceful admission of Meredith to Ole Miss. Barnett had lost confidence in his ability to restrain the extremists, who were vowing to use all means, including violence, to stop Meredith from integrating Ole Miss. Barnett was a staunch segregationist, but he did not want to destroy the university or plunge the state into a second civil war. Thus, while continuing to assure white Mississippians that their schools would never be integrated under his administration, he opened negotiations with the Kennedys to find a face-saving way to avoid violence. The plan that he and Robert Kennedy contrived was for Meredith and his escort to enter the campus, where they would be confronted by Barnett, who, acting as registrar of the university as well as governor of the state, would again deny admission. At that time the marshals were to draw their guns—and an important negotiating point that Barnett insisted on was that *all* the marshals would draw their guns—after which Barnett would step aside, thus giving him a face-saving photo opportunity for displaying his heroic defiance before a national television audience.[2]

As Meredith's caravan approached Oxford, Barnett and Lt. Governor Paul Johnson, who were both on the campus, began to worry that the state's small security force was inadequate to provide security in the face of growing armed opposition from diehard segregationists. Two hundred highway patrolmen guarded entrances to the campus, but as they checked autos to make sure no armed persons entered, their own guns were in their cars. As the time approached for Meredith's arrival, nearly 2,500 people, many of them armed, were swarming around the campus, and about 1,000 students stood near the gate where Meredith was expected to arrive. The FBI had intelligence that 19 Klansmen from Louisiana were already in Oxford, blending into the crowd. Lieutenants of the KKK's Imperial Wizard Robert Shelton were also in the crowd preparing reports to Alabama Klansmen who were awaiting the signal to join them. Mississippi Citizens' Council Chief William Simmons was surveying the crowd for signs of what he had hoped for all along: massive resistance by a united white population against federal intervention that threatened Mississippian's segregated way of life.

But Barnett and Johnson saw something else when they surveyed the scene. They saw what could easily become a killing field in which the badly outnumbered and outgunned highway patrolmen would be no match for the large and angry crowd. Johnson had toured the area in a police car and had seen firsthand the swelling, armed crowd. William Goodman, a Jackson attorney, was also on hand and recalled the scene: "There were so many scary people around who had come to town to see the show, armed with hunting rifles, shotguns, hatchets and bricks." Johnson was the first to call Robert Kennedy to call off the arranged confrontation and registration. "We cannot assure that those people or someone maybe hotheaded won't start shooting," he reported. "We've got some hotheaded people in this state who are in this group and we've got to have sufficient time to move them." Here was an official acknowledgment that Barnett and Johnson, who had repeatedly pandered to those "hotheaded" Mississippians, could not control them. Kennedy instructed Johnson to find some way to control the crowd and told him that he was ordering the marshals to bring Meredith onto the campus for registration that day. At 4:15 P.M., with the caravan just minutes outside the Ole Miss campus, Barnett called Robert Kennedy with a final appeal to turn back. "There is liable to be a hundred people killed here," he asserted. Perhaps remembering his bold pledges to "never" allow the desegregation of schools, Barnett added, "A lot of people are going to get killed. It would be embarrassing for me." Appalled that the governor's primary concern was his political embarrassment, RFK replied that that was not what he was feeling. Nonetheless, he was convinced that Barnett could not protect Meredith and keep order, so he ordered the caravan to turn around and return to Memphis.[3] Once more Meredith's hopes had been dashed, and his faith in the federal government to protect him weakened.

John and Robert Kennedy understood that events in Oxford were pushing them ever closer to exercising the political option they wanted to avoid: sending federal troops to Ole Miss. Neither Barnett nor Meredith would back down from his entrenched position; the former, despite court orders, was clinging to his states' rights position, and the latter was determined to desegregate Ole Miss. In a 1964 oral history, the attorney general maintained that it was Barnett who forced the administration to send in troops:

Lt. Governor Paul Johnson denies admission to James Meredith.
© Flip Schulke/Corbis

What I was trying to avoid...was having to send troops and trying to avoid having a federal presence in Mississippi. In my judgment, what [Barnett] was trying to accomplish was the avoidance
of integration at the University of Mississippi, number one. And if
he couldn't do that, to be forced to do it by our heavy hand; and his
preference was with troops....He had people pulling and pushing
at him from so many different directions that, I think, he just got
himself into a bigger and bigger box. He eventually pulled me in
with him.[4]

For the crowds back at Ole Miss, news that Meredith's registration had once again been thwarted was cause for celebration.
Knowing nothing of Barnett's deal with the Kennedys, the staunch

segregationists viewed the standoff as a triumph, a battle victory that meant the war against the federal government could be won. For most Ole Miss students, the 75 percent or more who did not go to the gate, even out of curiosity, it meant that their attention could return to what they most wanted: another academic year in which to pursue their own dreams unbothered by outside distractions. More immediately, it meant that they could enjoy a big football weekend.

Ole Miss students reflected the political views of their parents, and that meant that they accepted segregation and states' rights without serious examination and reflection. That is what they had been taught. Ross Barnett, Jr., the governor's son, an Ole Miss graduate and a young lawyer in Jackson, probably spoke for a majority of students when he explained that his father's views were consistent with those of Mississippians in general:

> The majority of [white] people of the state of Mississippi felt the same way my father did. The number-one plank in his platform was segregation of the races. That was all we knew down here. If you're used to doing something for years and years and years, and all of a sudden you've got to change, when change comes, regardless of what the change is, it disturbs people.[5]

Though many students accepted prevailing white attitudes toward segregation, not all gave their support uncritically. Certainly when defiance of a federal court order threatened their educations, many called for restraint and moderation rather than blind defiance. Just as one can see both continuity and change reflected in intergenerational attitudes and actions within the civil rights movement, one can also see continuity and change between Ole Miss students and their parents.

In September 1962, Ole Miss students were hardly consumed with politics, but they did worry about what politics might do to them and their futures. Twenty years after Meredith's admission, John Corlew, president of the student body in 1964–1965, reflected on his priorities at the time. He stated that he was far more interested in the annual Welcome Rebel party and other beginning-of-semester events than he was in segregation. Trent Lott remembers that he and his Sigma Nu fraternity brothers were more concerned about personal matters and campus activities than they were about desegregation. That said, the Meredith case did raise at least one very important issue that no student could ignore: the specter of the university losing its accreditation. It had happened once before, in 1930, when Governor Theodore Bilbo had fired three college presidents and scores of professors who opposed his plans to reorganize the state's colleges and universities. SACS had suspended the accreditation of all colleges in Mississippi because of undue political meddling in academic affairs. Students feared that Barnett's current meddling would once again result in the loss of accreditation.

When students did comment on Meredith's move to integrate Ole Miss, they frequently expressed resentment over the "political influence" that he marshaled for the effort. Some merely accepted Barnett's version of events and believed that he was not qualified, that he was seeking special treatment, and that a white applicant with his profile would be rejected. When referring to Meredith white Mississippians frequently pointed out, as Trent Lott did, that he was a *29-year-old Air Force veteran*, as if that alone should raise red flags. The implication was that such a person had no business entering a student body dominated by 18- to 22-year-olds. Thus, his motives for enrollment were suspect—surely it was not simply to get an education. Lott also contended that Meredith applied to Ole Miss "with heavy political backing" and with a political agenda: if successful, his application to all-white Ole Miss "would force full integration of the state's educational system."[6]

Lott's observation was partially true, but it told only part of the story. Meredith did reluctantly enlist the support of the NAACP and the U.S. Justice Department after Governor Barnett refused his application and wrote him "that he was not welcome at Ole Miss." But, the decision to integrate Ole Miss was Meredith's and his alone. As Charles Evers recalled, "Truth is, Medgar wasn't itching to integrate Ole Miss after what he'd been through in 1954, after whites had sent Clyde Kennard to prison and Clennon King to the loony bin. And Medgar knew that James Meredith didn't make the ideal test case.... [Meredith] made up his own mind to integrate Ole Miss."[7] Lott was right, at least in part, about Meredith's political aims; in addition to getting an education that would open doors for him personally, he sought to open Mississippi schools to all qualified students without regard to race. Like Lott, Meredith knew that an Ole Miss education was a prerequisite to certain positions of power. In explaining his choice of colleges,

Lott noted that Ole Miss had also been the choice of all of the state's governors and state-wide officials in the 1950s. What Lott failed to mention was that his own admission, as well as that of all the other students, was politically shaped as well. The state political machine had ensured that white students alone would enjoy the benefits of an Ole Miss education. In a state with a more than 40 percent black population, white students would have faced greater competition for admission if the school had not been segregated.

For the 2,000 or more students who traveled to Jackson for the football game against Kentucky, the weekend represented an escape from thoughts of desegregation, campus disturbances, and federal court orders. They reveled in the round of parties that always took place in hotels, motels, homes, and country clubs when Ole Miss played in the state capital. And, they delighted in cheering the Rebels on to their second win of what would become one of the school's best season's ever: a perfect record, an SEC championship, a third-place national ranking, and a Sugar Bowl victory. But, they could not escape signs of an impending crisis over their school's desegregation.

Outsiders in attendance noted what they considered to be signs of defiance throughout the stadium on game night, but to Ole Miss students there was nothing unusual at all until halftime. Reporters from outside the state interpreted the presence of Confederate flags and Confederate "keppie caps" as ominous displays related to the political crisis. But, to Ole Miss students, those were expressions of school spirit proudly displayed at every game. After all, the team's nickname was the "Rebels." Moreover, the marching band wore "keppie hats" as part of their uniform. At every game rebel flags, big and small, were everywhere, and "Dixie" was sung with gusto. For students, those were not political statements, any more than was LSU's roaring tiger or Georgia's snarling Bulldog.

In a region where football is a holy ritual, Southeastern Conference games are played within an electric atmosphere, especially when a nationally ranked team is playing at home. But, there was an unusual charge inside Memorial Stadium in Jackson, Mississippi, on the night of September 29, 1962. During the first half, the University of Mississippi football team demonstrated in their game against the University of Kentucky that they were indeed the powerhouse that had

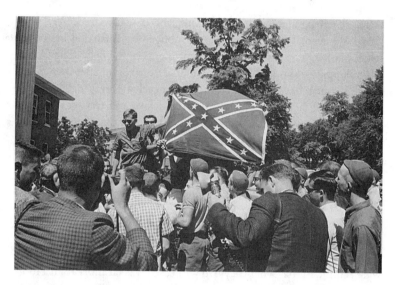

Confederate flag-waving students protesting U.S. Marshals' support of James Meredith.

© *Bettmann/Corbis*

brought them near the top of national polls. So it was not surprising that the roaring crowd of 43,000 was on its feet to greet the Rebels as they returned to the field for the second half. But the crowd's attention was not directed toward the players, rather it was focused on Governor Ross Barnett, who was standing at the 50-yard line in front of a microphone. The public address announcer directed the fans to the scoreboard, where words of a newly commissioned state fight song were displayed. Expressing white Mississippians' contempt for Justice Department mandates and federal court orders, it was entitled, "Never, No, Never."

> Never, Never, Never, No-o-o Never Never Never,
> We will not yield an inch of any field,
> Fix us another toddy, ain't yieldin' to nobody,
> Ross's standin' like Gibraltar, he shall never falter,
> Ask us what we say, it's to hell with Bobby K,
> Never shall our emblem go from Colonel Reb to Old Black
> Joe.

After the rousing singing of the song, the crowd roared, "We want Ross! We want Ross!" The governor obliged by thrusting his raised fist above his head and echoed the sentiments of the fight song: "I love Mississippi," he shouted in a voice hoarse from recent speeches. Then, in what must have been the shortest speech he ever delivered, he added, "I love her people! Our customs! I love and respect our heritage!"[8] The crowd got the message: Ross was standing firm on states' rights, regardless of the court order.

Barnett's halftime performance made a different impression on many Mississippians who later reflected on it. One Ole Miss student recalled, "It was like a big Nazi rally. Yes, it was just the way Nuremberg must have felt." A Jackson attorney thought that it was more like a spectacle staged in the Colosseum with tens of thousands of Romans screaming as the Christians and the lions did battle. Whatever the image they carried with them from the stadium, Ole Miss students were reminded that what they had witnessed was far more than a football game—it was a call to war.

While Ross Barnett moved the crowd, the crowd moved him. Earlier on Saturday he had had three telephone conversations with the Kennedys trying to work out yet another plan to register Meredith without violence. Barnett told the president that he was in a "horrible situation," referring to the pressure that extreme segregationists had put him under to defy the court order. He did not mention that he had stoked that extremism throughout his campaign for governor and during every day of his administration. President Kennedy explained his position: "Well, now here's my problem. . . . Listen, I didn't put him [Meredith] in the university, but on the other hand, under the Constitution, I have to carry out that order and I don't want to do it in any way that causes difficulty for you or to anyone else. But I've got to do it. Now, I'd like your help in doing that." Barnett countered with his own constitutional defense: "You know what I'm up against, Mr. President. I took an oath, you know, to abide by the laws of this state, and our Constitution here and the Constitution of the United States. I'm on the spot here, you know." Kennedy summed up their relative positions: "The problem is, Governor, that I got my responsibility, just like you have yours." Finally, just hours before the kickoff of the football game, the two men reached an agreement, known as the "decoy plan." Meredith would register on Monday in Jackson, not in Oxford, as most expected and where no doubt angry crowds would once again assemble. Barnett and Johnson would be at Ole Miss "standing heroically at the entrance to the university." Barnett would then feign surprise upon "learning" that Meredith had been registered at Jackson but, nonetheless, would allow him to begin classes on Tuesday under protection of the Highway Patrol. Barnett had reluctantly agreed to the "decoy plan;" in the private, rational exchanges with the president and attorney general, it seemed to be his only course of action. Now, however, buoyed by the cheering throng at Memorial Stadium, things looked different. After the game, an adviser suggested that he just admit Meredith and be done with it, but Barnett replied, "I can't do it. Did you see the crowd?"[9] Thus, as he prepared to return to Oxford to again deny Meredith admission on Monday, he called Robert Kennedy and told him that he would not go through with the decoy plan.

Upon learning of Barnett's rejection of the deal, President Kennedy prepared to implement the plan that he had hoped to avoid: sending federal troops to Mississippi to execute the court order, ensure Meredith's safety, and prevent bloodshed. Of course, President Eisenhower had established a precedent for the use of troops for school desegregation, and President Kennedy followed that precedent as to both the composition and the number of the forces that would be committed. Accordingly, he ordered into action the task force that he had previously instructed Army General Creighton Abrams to organize. He immediately dispatched 500 men from the 720th Military Police Battalion at Fort Hood to a staging area in Memphis, and he signed an executive order federalizing the Mississippi National Guard. He worried about the loyalty of the guardsmen, but he thought it best to have local men at the vanguard of his military response. His worries were confirmed when General Maxwell Taylor called several unit commanders of the National Guard to gauge how their men would react if they were called upon to escort Meredith onto the Ole Miss campus. One commander bluntly told Taylor that he personally would lead his men out the door and out of the Army. He predicted that it would be an exodus of historical proportions. While Kennedy's military response paralleled that of President Eisenhower in 1957 during the Little Rock crisis, he worried about the outcome. Foremost in his worries was whether or not the 11,000-member Mississippi National Guard would obey his orders.

Oblivious to secret deals and troop preparations, students returned to Oxford on Sunday. As they drove toward the campus, they saw some puzzling and disturbing signs that the crisis that they had hoped had passed was reaching a critical stage. Trent Lott recalled his drive back to Ole Miss. With echoes of the governor's halftime words in his mind, he worried that some "accepted Barnett's words as a battle cry, or at least a gesture of defiance." Further, he was aware that the remarks reached "millions of Southerners" who tuned into the game on radio or watched highlights on television. When he and his girlfriend drove north on U.S. Highway 51, she observed that many of the cars headed toward the campus had out-of-state license plates, especially from Texas, Louisiana, and Oklahoma. Apparently Barnett's speech was indeed a battle cry for white supremacists across the South who had pledged to aid their Mississippi brothers and sisters in the fight to keep Ole Miss segregated.

The day broke crisp and clear over the sleepy Ole Miss campus on Sunday, September 30. With at least half of the student body out of town, there was little activity during the morning hours. Political science professor Russell Barrett took advantage of the quiet hours to work in his office, drafting a paper he had agreed to write. About noon, as he left the campus he stopped and chatted with anthropology professor Paul Hahn about the Meredith case, wondering what the next step would be. Hahn voiced concern over the large number of "outside toughs" who were already in Oxford, some of whom were actually on the campus. Both expressed hope that the Justice Department would do nothing that day, especially not bring Meredith onto the campus. After making the drive back to his house in Oxford, Barrett commented to his wife, "There sure are a lot of bums in town." What disturbed Barrett most as the incoming traffic picked up in the early afternoon was that many of the cars, instead of containing returning students, were occupied by nothing but men, often four or five in a single car. Moreover, many of the cars hailed from outside Mississippi, an unusual sight on a typical Sunday in the small, lazy town.[10]

That morning Oxford ministers, worried about an impending showdown between the federal and state governments, repeated their calls for "Christian behavior." Rector Duncan Gray of St. Peter's Episcopal Church had been an outspoken and consistent voice of moderation, as had all but one of Oxford's ministers. While many preachers

Rioting at Ole Miss—Sunday night, September 30, 1962.
© *Bettmann/Corbis*

in the rest of the state had labeled civil rights activists as "outside agitators" and had banned them from their churches, the Oxford ministers had preached messages of justice and Christian forbearance. Gray's sermon that day rejected Barnett's claim that the state's cause in the Meredith case was "righteous and just." While conceding that Barnett and those Mississippians who shared his views were no doubt sincere, Gray stated his own position: "But, in the name of reason and in the name of Christian standards of freedom and justice, I ask you to consider the fact that *no university in the world would defend this position rationally, and no Christian Church in the world would defend it morally...*." Presbyterian minister Murphey C. Wilds objected to the notion of Mississippi sovereignty that was emblazoned on bumper stickers and billboards across the state, reminding his parishioners that "God is sovereign."[11]

At about 3:30 P.M., the quiet peace of the Ole Miss campus was shattered by an unusual sound: the roar of military transport planes arriving at the Oxford airport. The small, municipal airport had heretofore rarely accommodated anything larger than two-engine DC-3's. In fact, when the Ole Miss football team flew to away games, frequently two DC-3's would ferry the squad to Memphis, where the players would deplane and board a larger plane for the flight to the final destination. Now a number of large military transport planes descended on the tiny airport with their cargoes of federal marshals. In fact, most of the 536 law enforcement officers were not marshals, but an assortment of men who had undergone special riot training programs. The force consisted of 123 deputy marshals, 316 border patrolmen, and 97 prison guards from federal penitentiaries. By a little after 4 P.M. seven Army transport trucks rumbled onto campus, and the federal officers took up positions encircling the Lyceum Building.

The presence of the federal marshals around the Lyceum became the focal point for protestors, who by 4 P.M. numbered about 400, but, as in any battle, there was much confusion that led to conflicting reports about the size and composition of the crowd. One reporter estimated that the crowd was about 2,000 at the beginning and grew to almost 4,000 at its peak. Professor Barrett, who was on the campus for much of the rioting, thought that a more accurate guess might be a couple hundred at the outset and 2,000 at its largest. Whatever the actual number was in fact, it was very large considering that the student body numbered only about 4,500. But who were the rioters? Again, reports vary. One reporter estimated that at the beginning almost 95 percent were students, while Professor Barrett thought that about two thirds were students. It was clear to him that as the evening progressed, the percentage of students declined steadily. Deputy Marshal Duane Caldwell estimated that by 8 P.M., "youths of student age were in the minority." The most objective estimate of the percentage of students in the rioting mob comes from the number of students arrested during the evening. Fewer than one sixth of those arrested were Ole Miss students.[12] That said, the number of students actively involved is not a good gauge of student body attitudes about Meredith's admission. While much of the student body was not directly involved in the riot itself that evening, many did in fact agree with the cause of the rioters.

University officials did their best to maintain order among the students, but Chancellor Williams had been excluded from the decision to abandon the decoy plan and bring Meredith to Ole Miss on Sunday instead of to Jackson on Monday. He and his staff had developed a plan for keeping the peace on campus, but they were caught off guard and unable to implement it. Their exclusion underscored the fact that the matter of integrating Ole Miss had been taken from the university's hand and had become a political football between the state and federal governments. Nonetheless, Williams did what he could, personally addressing students gathered in front of the Lyceum, urging them to return to their dorms and fraternity and sorority houses. Leaders of student government and presidents of Greek societies also tried to persuade students to stay away from the growing crowd.

Meanwhile, James Meredith had been brought onto the campus in an unmarked federal car and ensconced in Baxter Hall at the western end of the campus, far from the protests. Earlier in the day, when the first federal troops arrived at Millington Naval Air Station near Memphis, Meredith for the first time believed that his admission was in fact going to take place. His strategy from the beginning had hinged on federal government support, and with the arrival of troops he knew that he had that support. After arriving on campus, Meredith began the long wait until Monday morning for his scheduled registration.

Worried about the ugly scene developing on campus, football coach Johnny Vaught told his team to stay away from the Lyceum. He convened the players in the basement of Miller Hall, the dormitory exclusively built to house the team, late in the afternoon as the crowd began taunting the federal officials at the Lyceum. After reviewing film of the Kentucky game of the previous night and discussing the upcoming game against the University of Houston, Vaught addressed the situation on campus. "I don't know what's going to happen," he said, "and you don't know what will happen. Ross Barnett sure as hell doesn't know what is going to happen." With that he instructed the players to stay away from the gathering crowds. The meeting ended around 7:30, and, within minutes most of the players had, despite the coach's admonition, walked over to the crowd to see what was happening. They stood on the steps of Peabody Hall and in front of Fulton Chapel, the two buildings closest to the Lyceum. They arrived in time to see the crowd throw rocks at the federal marshals and turn over government vehicles. They saw bricks, bottles, and pieces of pipe hit and wound marshals, prompting Chief U.S. Marshal James McShane to give the order to disperse the crowd with tear gas. With the firing of tear gas at just before 8 p.m., the battle was joined. The firing also sent the curious football players sprinting back to Miller Hall, where coaches took roll and locked the team in for the night. One player was missing.

The marshals were left to fight the crowd alone because beginning at about 7:30 the Mississippi Highway Patrolmen had withdrawn from the campus. Seeing the patrolmen pull out, the crowd cheered, interpreting the withdrawal as a green light from the state to attack the feds. Colonel Tom Birdsong was commander of the state troopers, and he explained to Deputy Attorney General Nicholas Katzenbach that his men had fulfilled their duty to escort the marshals onto the campus and that he had told the crowd that that was the extent of the state's duty. State Senator Tom Yarborough, chief of Barnett's delegation on campus, confirmed to McShane and Katzenbach that the Highway Patrol was leaving. "You have occupied this University and now you can have it," he declared. He delivered what would become the postbattle position of the governor and his supporters: "What happens from now on is the responsibility of the Federal Government." With the patrolmen gone, the marshals were indeed in a precarious position, outnumbered and probably outgunned. Moreover, the patrolmen abandoned their posts at the campus entrances, providing a clear path for outsiders to enter the campus and battle the feds.

At about the same time, Governor Barnett delivered a radio broadcast from Jackson, a mixed message calling for order, yet also expressing continued defiance. Like Yarborough, he placed responsibility for the night's events on the federal government. "I have just been informed by the Attorney General of the United States," he announced, "that Meredith has today been placed on the campus of the University of Mississippi by means of government helicopters and is accompanied by Federal officers." He then pleaded with the crowd to avoid violence while at the same time inflaming passions by depicting himself and the state as victims of a tyrannical occupation force. "Surrounded on all sides by the armed forces and oppressive power of the United States of America," he cried, "my courage and my convictions do not waver. My heart still says 'never,' but my calm judgment abhors the bloodshed that would follow." Then, reiterating his remarks that had inflamed the crowd at Memorial Stadium the previous night, he continued, "I love Mississippi. I love her people, I love the 10,000 good Mississippians in the National Guard who have now been federalized and required to oppose me and their own people." He closed with what could be interpreted by the crowd at Ole Miss as an invitation to defy federal authority. Addressing federal officials, he said, "You are trampling on the sovereignty of this great state and depriving it of every vestige of honor and respect as a member of the United States. You are destroying the Constitution of this great nation. May God have mercy on your souls."[13]

Upon learning that the Highway Patrol was withdrawing from the campus, Robert Kennedy called Katzenbach at the Lyceum and instructed him to tell Yarborough that if he did not order the Highway Patrol back to their posts, the president, who was about to deliver a national television address, would tell the world about the many secret telephone conversations that Barnett had had with the Kennedy Administration. Unaware of those talks, Yarborough was confused. So the attorney general called Barnett with the same message, and Barnett instructed Yarborough to bring the troopers back. At the same time the scene in front of the Lyceum was taking a dangerous turn. Shortly after Barnett's speech, someone hurled a Molotov cocktail that exploded among the marshals, and another threw a rock that knocked a marshal down. McShane ordered his men to load their tear-gas guns and prepare to disperse the crowd.

Just minutes after McShane gave the order to fire, President Kennedy went on television to address the nation about events at Ole Miss, but he wished specifically to speak to the students there. He had originally planned to speak at 6 P.M. but delayed his remarks, fearing that they might inflame passions more than calm them. Knowing that white Mississippians had a higher regard for the law than for civil rights, he justified his actions as a defense of the rule of law. He declared, "Americans are free, in short, to disagree with the law—but not to disobey it. For in a government of laws, and not of men, no man, however prominent or powerful, and no mob, however unruly or boisterous, is entitled to defy a court order." Kennedy then saluted the eight southern states that now admitted students "regardless of race," but he refused to blame Mississippians for failing to follow in their footsteps. Mississippi was not to blame, he said, but all Americans share the responsibility of the failure of improving race relations in the country. The president closed by appealing directly to Ole Miss students and challenging them to do the unexpected:

> You have a great tradition to uphold, a tradition of honor and cour-
> age, won on the field of battle and on the gridiron as well as the
> university campus. You have a new opportunity to show that you
> are men of patriotism and integrity.... The eyes of the nation and
> all the world are upon you and upon all of us, and the honor of your
> university and the state are in the balance. I am certain that the
> great majority of the students will uphold that honor.[14]

As the nation began to receive reports of the rioting at Ole Miss, the early news was not that of honor, but of mayhem. Incensed by the tear gas, the crowd, now numbering perhaps 2,000, attacked on sev- eral fronts: turning over and burning federal vehicles, beating "outside" journalists, and advancing toward the federal marshals at the Lyceum. Without a leader and a coordinated plan, the rioters struck at targets of opportunity while staying out of range of the marshal's canisters. Just before 9 P.M., former U.S. Major General Edwin Walker appeared on campus, and for some, he represented the leader that the mob needed. In 1957 Walker had commanded the troops that President Eisenhower sent to enforce the desegregation order at Little Rock's Central High School. However, he resigned his commission in 1961 after being reprimanded on several occasions for indoctrinating his troops with right-wing propaganda, including accusations that Presi- dent Truman and Eleanor Roosevelt had Communist leanings. From his home in Texas, Walker became obsessed with the Meredith case, and on September 26, 1962, called for volunteers all over the South to rally behind Governor Barnett to stop the desegregation of Ole Miss. He told a radio audience on Shreveport, Louisiana, station KWKH that, "I have been on the other side in such situations in a place called Little Rock, and I was on the wrong side. This time I will be in... Mis- sissippi, on the right side." Now on the Ole Miss campus, Walker ral- lied the crowd in the early moments of the riot. Addressing them from the base of the Confederate monument, he said, "I want to compli- ment you all on the protest you're making." He roared, "You have a right to protest under the Constitution; any bloodshed here tonight is on the hands of the federal government.... Don't let up now. You may lose this battle, but you will have to be heard." Walker whipped the crowd into a fury. When Rev. Duncan Gray arrived alongside Walker and urged the crowd to go home, someone reached up, grabbed the minister, and threw him to the ground. When someone shouted that Gray should not be hurt because he was a minister, the person holding him down retorted, "Let's kill the son-of-a-bitch."[15] The crowd was in a frenzy and wanted blood. Fortunately for Gray, federal blood was the prize.

The battle hung in the balance during the next two hours, from about 9 to around 11 P.M., as marshals tried to bring the crowd under control with too few men and ammunition. The crowd made a series of advances on the Lyceum, one time behind a commandeered fire truck, only to be driven back by tear gas, but the supply was dwindling. As the rioting intensified, both federal and state officials feared that hundreds would die. Within an hour of firing the first canisters, the marshals were running out of tear gas, and the surging crowd began to open fire. One marshal was shot through the leg and carried into the Lyceum, which had, as it had been a hundred years before during the Civil War, again become a hospital. Then, after a patrolman was badly hurt, the state troopers again left the campus upon Barnett's orders. No federal troops were close to campus; indeed, it would be hours before the first U.S. Army troops would arrive.

The campus was quickly transformed into a war zone where noncombatants as well as combatants were at risk. Indeed, shortly after the mob started firing on the marshals, Paul Guilhard, a French journalist who had just entered the campus and was making his way toward the riot scene, was felled by a bullet. And, Ray Gunter, a local resident who stood on the fringe of the campus about 220 yards east of the Lyceum watching the spectacle unfold, was hit by a stray bullet. No one was safe.

Around 10 P.M. Deputy Attorney General Nicholas Katzenbach called President Kennedy and requested federal troops. Gunfire was spreading, and he feared that the number of deaths could soar. Although the Mississippi National Guard had been federalized, only the local contingent of 67 guardsmen was available for immediate duty. Captain Murry Falkner, nephew of Nobel laureate William Faulkner, received the call from Katzenbach and, as commander of the

Oxford-based Troop E, Second Squadron, 108th Armored Cavalry Regiment of the Mississippi National Guard, he prepared his troops for battle. The men had had only a few hours of anti-riot training, and many of them were sympathetic to the rioters' cause of segregation and states' rights. But, they were also soldiers who had received a direct order from their commanding officer to move out. Katzenbach had ordered Falkner to leave their live ammunition behind in the armory, fearing that more civilians would be killed. So the force of 67 unarmed Mississippi guardsmen with divided loyalties piled into three jeeps and three trucks and moved out to the campus. As long as men have fought in wars, people have speculated about their motivation. Do they put their lives on the line because of the cause, be it revolution, rebellion, world domination, or some other abstraction, or does the fighting itself provide motivation for them to stay on the field of battle at the risk of their lives? The ambivalent guardsmen were about to be tested. One of the troops in a truck that night was Loyd Gunter, whose regular job was that of a checkout clerk at Kroger supermarket. He recalled that as the convoy rumbled toward the campus, he heard one of his comrades say, "I'll tell you one damn thing, when we get out there, I'll get out there and help them sombitches throw bricks!"[16] Gunter hastened to add that that sentiment was not shared by all the soldiers, but it indicated the divided opinions.

When the convoy entered the campus, it came under attack as the crowd threw bricks and stones at the jeeps and trucks. Gunter remembered well the greeting that they received: the "grove was full of people hollering and cussing—I never heard such language in my life. They were throwing bricks, chains, bottles, everything they could get their hands on. When we ran the blockade, we wound up getting 28 men injured going in. Any of us who didn't know which side they was on, that made up their dam[sic] mind right there." Corporal Harold Antwine recalled that both windows of his jeep were smashed. Worse, a concrete slab slammed into the passenger side, almost knocking Captain Falkner out of the vehicle and breaking his arm. Falkner ordered the men to drive through the crowd to reach the besieged marshals at the Lyceum. Under fire from the mob, the guardsmen's divided loyalties vanished. As Falkner put it: "If there had been any doubt as to whether the men would follow me,...there was none now.

I was indubitably sure I had their support. A person loose in that mob, wearing a uniform, would have been dead. Now we were all concerned with a matter of self-preservation." He added, "It's hard to feel brotherly love toward someone who is trying to kill you."[17]

When the convoy finally reached the Lyceum, Falkner grabbed a bullhorn and tried to address the crowd. After all, he had attended Ole Miss, and several of his men were current Ole Miss students. "We're from Mississippi," Falkner shouted. "We live here. Now y'all get out of here." The response was a hail of stones, curses, and Molotov cocktails. But the guardsmen stood their ground. With nothing more than their courage and 15 fixed bayonets, that small band of guardsmen placed itself between the mob and the marshals. Without question, the guardsmen prevented a wholesale bloodbath.

In addition to the guardsmen, the lone football player who had not returned to Miller Hall now stepped forward to challenge the crowd. If the football team had been polled prior to knowing the identity of the one missing teammate, the response would no doubt have been unanimous: Buck Randall. Far from the biggest guy on the team, Buck was one of the toughest. About 5'10" and 210 pounds, he was a solid, compact hitting machine who played hard-nosed football on offense as a fullback and on defense as a linebacker. Buck loved contact, and he never backed down from a challenge. He was a player's player. So it was little wonder that Buck was somewhere near the Lyceum while the rest of the team was locked in Miller Hall. Why Buck was there is a matter of speculation. Perhaps he was curious. Or maybe he could not resist being near the action. But, he was there when University Chaplain Wofford Smith spotted him at about 10 P.M. around the Lyceum and told James McShane that Buck was a football star. McShane asked Buck to go out onto the steps of the Lyceum and try to disperse the crowd—perhaps they would listen to someone they respected. Buck agreed. At first the crowd seemed to listen. He told them that they needed to stop their actions, that people were going to get killed, and that they needed to leave. One heckler shouted, "Propaganda! Let's charge the building again!" Another boldly said, "Let's pull this son of a bitch down off of there." To that, all Buck's fighting instincts boiled up and he shouted back, "Bring your ass on. If you want some of me, just come on!"[18] No one took him on. Randall was not the only student leader who tried to calm the crowd that night, but, like the Mississippi guardsmen, he placed himself between the mob and the marshals and tried to bring calm and order.

In an incident that threatened armed conflict between state and federal officers, Lt. Governor Paul Johnson exercised cool judgment and exhibited considerable courage to keep the riot from escalating to all-out civil war. Johnson had been a stalwart in standing with Governor Barnett in preventing Meredith from registering. And, when he followed Barnett as governor, he governed Mississippi very much in the Barnett-demagogue model. But, for a key moment during the riot, Johnson showed courage and restraint to prevent further violence. After withdrawing from the fray, a group of state troopers decided to join the fight against the marshals and were organizing to return to the campus for the confrontation when Johnson arrived. Having learned of the plot, the lieutenant governor knew that such an action could escalate the riot into a full-fledged war between federal and state forces. Therefore, he stood before the troopers and told them to stand down, and he reminded them that they had taken oaths to maintain law and order. By persuading them to abandon their scheme, Johnson joined the guardsmen and Randall as Mississippians who faced their fellow citizens to preserve life.

The arrival of 165 more National Guardsmen shortly after midnight represented a turning point as members of Troop G and a howitzer battery of the 108th Cavalry's Second Squadron began to put the rioters on the defensive. Then, just before 2:00 A.M. the first U.S. Army troops, a detachment of the 503rd Military Police, arrived on campus and the rioters began to disperse, with many leaving the campus altogether. While a few individuals and small groups continued to cause disturbances on campus and in Oxford, most vanished into the night. The Ole Miss riot was over. Two people had been killed—neither Paul Guilhard nor Ray Gunter survived his gunshot wounds—over 300 hundred wounded, and more than 200 arrested. The campus looked like a battlefield, with smoke rising from burned vehicles and debris scattered all over the area in front of the Lyceum.

Through it all, James Meredith had remained in his Baxter Hall dormitory room at the western edge of the campus. He could hear gunshots but was unaware of the events unfolding at the Lyceum. He later recalled that when the riot began, he was putting away his things

Aftermath of the riot.
© Bettmann/Corbis

and making up his bed, much as any newly arrived student would do. He went to bed around 10 but was awakened several times by the "noise and shooting outside." It would not be until Monday morning that he would learn the outcome of the battle between a few hundred federal marshals and National Guardsmen, who fought to ensure his safety, and a couple thousand whites who were equally determined to keep him out of Ole Miss.

CHAPTER 7

....

Mission Accomplished

Ole Miss Integrated?

....

...the most segregated Negro in the world.
James Meredith, 1963

....

A s James Meredith walked to class, the security detail assigned
to him swung into action. Two federal marshals preceded him,
two flanked him, and two walked behind. On the street opposite the sidewalk where he walked, a convoy of four Army jeeps crept
alongside carrying a dozen soldiers in full battle regalia with fixed bayonets; they scanned both sides of the street on the alert for any threat.
Out of sight were thousands of additional troops camped all over the
campus. Indeed, in fall 1962 Ole Miss looked more like an army base
than a university. At a peak strength of 20,000, soldiers outnumbered
students by about five to one. Troops were everywhere, bivouacked
on any plot of ground not covered by a building, including varsity and
intramural playing fields. Crack outfits like the 101st Airborne Division ran through the campus doing their daily physical training, shouting out their cadence: "Up the hill, Down the hill, Through the hill.
Airborne!" Troop carriers rumbled through the campus, transporting
squads of soldiers while helicopters buzzed overhead.

The militarized campus was the setting for James Meredith's experience as an Ole Miss student. First, it was a constant reminder that
his safety depended on such extraordinary measures. Almost daily
he received hate mail and death threats, and by the end of the first

U.S. troops patrol streets on Ole Miss campus.
© Bettmann/Corbis

semester he began to wonder if the costs were too great. The constant insults, jeers, and taunts from his fellow students had a cumulative effect, and, more worrisome to him, his family had come under attack. Late in the semester he learned that his parents' house in Kosciusko had been sprayed with bullets in a drive-by shooting. Second, all of the distractions he faced affected his academic performance. At mid-term he received a warning that his poor grades put his future at Ole Miss in jeopardy. So as the semester neared its end, Meredith announced that he was considering leaving Ole Miss. While he had anticipated resistance, what he encountered was far nastier and longer-lasting than he ever imagined.

The presence of troops was also the focus of lively debate for white students as they tried to make sense of the reality of an African American classmate. Their world had been turned upside down. The old verities that they had been taught were now called into question, and the promises of their leaders to safeguard the Mississippi Way had proved to be empty. Opinion was divided over a number of questions. Who was responsible for the riot? Ross Barnett? John Kennedy?

And, what should their attitudes be toward future black applicants? Even greater resistance? Acceptance? Prior to 1962, Ole Miss students had not been particularly engaged with social and political issues, content to go along with the traditions bequeathed to them. More than ever, they began to think for themselves as they asked questions and demanded answers.

....

James Meredith awoke at 6:30 on Monday morning, October 1, 1962, to a slight smell of tear gas in his dorm room in Baxter Hall. Unaware of the extent of rioting during the previous evening, he dressed for his long-awaited dream: his admission to the University of Mississippi. Accompanied by Justice Department attorney John Doar and Chief U.S. Marshal James McShane, he proceeded to the Lyceum Building to register for classes. As he approached the building that had been the center of the rioting, the Air Force veteran noted the "signs of strife and warfare" that were evident all around. Indeed, the border patrol car that he rode in was riddled with bullet holes, and its windows had been shot out. There was so much broken glass inside the car that Doar and McShane had to place blankets on the seats to avoid being cut. Signs of violence belied the eerie tranquility that surrounded Meredith's formal registration. He dutifully signed the required forms presented to him by Registrar Robert Ellis and completed his enrollment "without incident." He signed up for five courses: Colonial American History, American Political Parties, French Literature, English Literature, and Algebra. As a transfer student, he expected to finish his degree in three semesters, graduating at the end of the 1963 summer session with a major in history and a minor in political science. Upon leaving the building to attend his first class, a reporter asked him if he was now pleased, and Meredith, having by then learned of the deaths and injuries of the night before, replied, "This is no happy occasion." As he exited, he passed by a custodian, the first black person that he had seen on campus. He had wondered how black employees would react to him, and he got his first indication when the gentleman caught his eye and brushed the handle of his broom slightly against Meredith's hand in a gesture of support. It was an acknowledgment of what Meredith had done: opened the door of opportunity for all blacks.

James Meredith escorted to class by U.S. Marshals.
*Trikosko, Marion S. U.S. News & World Report Magazine Collection/Library of Congress,
Prints & Photographs Division [reproduction number, e.g., LU-U9–15739, frame 18]*

At 9 A.M. James Meredith took his seat in his first class, a course in Colonial American History. He was a few minutes late for the lecture on the English background to the colonization of North America, but the professor continued his lecture without acknowledging the historic significance of the moment. However, when several marshals who accompanied Meredith entered the classroom, the professor asked them to wait outside the room, establishing a precedent that was followed throughout Meredith's stay at Ole Miss. Only about a dozen students were in attendance; all greeted him in silence except for one girl, who said hello. He noticed that she was crying, but he assumed that it was because of the tear gas, because he, too, was crying for the same reason.

While Meredith attended his first classes, the Kennedy White House worried about how to bring lasting calm to the Ole Miss campus. In a White House conference between the president, his top advisors, and the attorney general, the mood was tense, with intermittent stabs at gallows humor. At one point, someone in the room said, "this reminds me a little bit of the Bay of Pigs." RFK hit upon the idea of seeking help from Ole Miss's popular football coach Johnny Vaught. Following up on the notion, he said to a secretary, "Let's see if we can get him." In the telephone conversation that followed, he asked Vaught to do what he could to "keep the situation calm." Vaught replied that he would. But, as Vaught recalled in his memoirs, "by Tuesday our Homecoming Game with Houston had become a pawn between state and federal forces.... It took a tremendous fight to keep the game...from being canceled." Vaught believed that there was a link between playing the game and restoring calm on the campus. "I felt it essential that the game be played," adding, "that it might be the key to getting the campus to settle down." After the game and an impressive Ole Miss victory, Vaught said that the players lifted the school on their shoulder pads that day. In fact, he titled that chapter of his memoirs, "Football Saves a School."[1] Whether or not the victory "saved" the school is debatable, but it was, no doubt, a timely diversion that redirected student focus from an extraordinary weekend of brickbats and tear gas to one of football and dreams of a national championship.

Meredith did not share those dreams. His struggle far transcended that of a football game. After attending two of his three classes on Monday (one was canceled because there was too much tear gas in the room), he returned to his room at Baxter Hall. As he reflected on the day's events, he had a profound sense of satisfaction at what he had accomplished, both for himself and for black Mississippians. The battle for admission had been a personal struggle as well as a fight for civil rights, and he had overcome the inner doubt that had plagued him over the question of whether he would "break before the system." Despite the administrative roadblocks put in his path over the past year and a half, the labyrinth of court proceedings, and the threats of violence that he had received, he had demonstrated great courage and perseverance, and, in the words of William Faulkner etched in stone on the campus, he had "not only endured, but prevailed." Meredith knew that the days and weeks and months ahead would not be easy as he faced the anger of white students who resented his presence and who blamed him for the rioting, but he believed that even if he did not graduate, he had done what he set out to do: establish for himself and for all black Mississippians the "privilege of choice." Now it was possible for one, regardless of growing up in white or black Mississippi, to enjoy the best that the state had to offer.

James Meredith faced far more than the challenges of a transfer student who began classes a week after the semester began. He was the only black student on a hostile campus and confronted daily the slights, insults, and taunts of white students who could not adjust to the new reality of an integrated university. But he viewed such behavior with perspective and maturity. Some students would step off the sidewalk when Meredith approached rather than share the same walkway with him, an act of supreme irony, Meredith thought, in a state where blacks had always stepped aside for whites. He also noticed racist and annoying symbols, such as a bumper sticker of "Colonel Rebel," the school mascot—a stylized kind of Rebel colonel—but this particular representation had his "face painted black, and with big, thick red lips. Down at the bottom of the sticker, was printed, 'Kennedy's new colonel.'" He later recalled that his encounters with students were mixed during his first days as a student. He wrote that "many—most, I would say, have been courteous, and the faculty members certainly have been." He heard the jeers and catcalls from some students, such as "We'll get you, nigger" and all that, but Meredith shrugged those off as people "just having a little fun." When he went to the cafeteria, not only did he sit alone, but students at other tables, in obvious protest to his presence, would stand up, turn around, and sit down facing the opposite direction from him. He tried to put such behavior in context, observing that it was not aimed at him personally but at the painful change that he represented. He did think it "tragic" that "they have to have this kind of fun about me, but many of them are children of the men who lead Mississippi today, and I would not expect them to act any other way. They have to act the way they do. I think I understand human nature enough to understand that."[2]

In addition to the distractions on campus that first semester, Meredith shouldered a far greater burden than that of the average undergraduate. His admission had attracted national attention, and he was flooded with mail from supporters and detractors alike. He personally responded to as many of the former as he could. He estimated that he received 200 letters a day throughout the semester. He received letters from African Americans who offered their encouragement for what they knew was a difficult time. One correspondent from New York wrote, "May I take this opportunity to thank you for the tremendous job that you are doing for all of us in the Negro race." She said that she and too many like her were afraid to become personally involved in issues such as this. "Thank God for people like you. Whenever you have moments of despair, please remember that thousands of Negro youngsters will have chances for better education because you, James Meredith, took a stand for the right and the truth." An African American from Chicago added, "It is because of brave Negroes like you, we have been able to progress.... I had often wondered what Negro would have the stamina to try to break Mississippi's segregation rule. It takes more than courage to do what you have done." Many others, like Mrs. Richard Johnson of New York, commented on his courage: "You've had great courage to get there, and you'll probably need a great deal more during the coming year."[3] Meredith was deeply touched by the hundreds of similar letters and tried to answer them, taking precious time from his studies.

Of course, he also received an abundance of hate mail. While he did not bother to respond to such letters, he did read some of them, not the kind of correspondence that most college students received. A sample of the venomous mail will suffice to give some idea of the sentiments expressed. One postcard was addressed to James H. Meredith [sic] "The Unwelcome Guest, University, Miss." The front read, "I've missed you." The inside showed a white man in a prone position holding a rifle with a scope attached and another nearby, with the caption: "but I'll take better aim in 1962." Others blamed him for the bloodshed at Ole Miss. "Isn't it really the truth that the Kennedys back you for this horrible thing you have done. You know the blood of Ole Miss will rest on your hands and the Kennedys. And the Bible says the soul that sinneth it shall die." A final example centers on the common stereotype of black males as sexual predators. One typical letter from someone who signed it as a "fed-up northerner," said, "From what I've seen of you niggers up north [sic], your peoples' idea of equality is the right to have sexual relations with any white woman you take a fancy to and to slash and stab any white man who refuses to take your nigger's shit and abuse, and who dares to stand up to you niggers."[4]

In addition to being flooded with mail, Meredith had other distractions. He had made national news and attained something that he did not seek: celebrity status. That new status brought further demands on his time. Mississippi blacks wrote or called him seeking advice on how they too could enter Ole Miss. In October he received a letter from Cleve McDowell, a senior at Jackson State, who was considering applying to the university's law school now that Meredith had set a precedent. The precedent was not dismantling the color barrier or bringing integration to Ole Miss, but it did mean that African Americans could gain access. Thus, McDowell asked Meredith about admissions procedures and financial aid, and he was particularly worried about what economic pressure whites might put on his parents in order to prevent his going to Ole Miss. Magazine and book publishers eager to capitalize on Meredith's experiences urged him to write accounts of his struggles. During October and November, he wrote a piece for the *Saturday Evening Post*, prepared another for *Esquire*, and made trips to New York to discuss a book deal with McGraw-Hill. All the while, he tried to maintain close contact with his wife Mary June, who was in college at Jackson State, and their 2-year-old son John Howard, who was living with his parents in Kosciusko. He called his wife three times a week and kept up a steady correspondence with her and his parents. Though he did the best he could to see them often, he regretted their being apart, commenting in the spring of 1963, "I don't think families should live apart."

As opposition to his presence at Ole Miss persisted, Meredith grew particularly concerned about his parents' safety. He was taken aback by the continuation of threats against him and his family. When he began the admissions process, he knew that there would be intense opposition from white supremacists, but he thought that it would subside within a couple weeks after his beginning classes. Thus he was greatly distressed when he learned that his father's house had become a target. He viewed attacks on his father as a grievous expression of injustice. He noted that his father had worked hard all his life, lived a good life, paid all his debts, never got into trouble, and was a good tax-paying citizen. But, Moses Meredith could not sleep in peace "without the danger of someone attacking him violently." James wrote of his father, "He has not gone to the University of Mississippi, or done any of the other things that the opposition might have been fighting about. Yet one night they fired into his house with shotguns."[5] Meredith blamed Mississippi politicians and their "system of laws" for creating the climate for such a thing to happen and for failing to pro-tect his father.

Little wonder that his grades suffered. On November 20, Mer-edith received his mid-term progress report along with a letter from the dean stating that his record for the first part of the semester was "unsatisfactory." Unlike other students who received similar reports, Meredith had to contend with his grades being made public. Upon hearing on the radio that James was not "passing" at Ole Miss, Mary June wrote him a letter expressing her concern and offering encourage-ment. She wrote, "I don't know why but I feel so bad. I suppose it is because I heard you were not passing at Ole Miss. This was on today's news. Of course I know you are capable. All I ask is that you do your very best. We cannot expect more. Just do your best." James was upset over the "extensive speculation" about his grades in the media and saw it as part of a campaign to discredit him and, by extension, all Mis-sissippi blacks. He saw all the talk about his grades as an attempt to shift attention away from the real issue, which he contended was the "right of access." He argued that "the right to fail is just as important as the right to succeed," so the real significance of what he had done at Ole Miss was in gaining access for blacks, not in attaining a particular grade point average.[6]

James Meredith was not alone in worrying about making the grade. About the same time he received his mid-term report, Ole Miss Administrators received a telegram from SACS, the university's accrediting agent and a body that the university had helped found. The telegram read in part that "all state institutions of higher learning of the State of Mississippi would be removed from the list of member schools at the next meeting of the Commission unless assurances were given that unwarranted procedures and political interferences of the State of Mississippi would be discontinued and assurances give that such procedures would not continue at the University of Mississippi or employed in the other institutions."[7] Students' worst fears were brought closer to reality. Ross Barnett had interfered in the university's governance, and now Ole Miss's accreditation was in jeopardy.

Despite his remarks about the right to fail, Meredith had no inten-tion of doing so. He redoubled his efforts and dramatically improved his academic performance over the rest of the semester. He put aside the writing projects and concentrated on his classes. He finished the semester with grades well above the grade point average necessary to continue as a student in good standing. The university itself did not fare so well in its attempts to improve its standing before SACS. Though university and state officials vowed never again to allow political interference in Ole Miss's governance, SACS gave the university an official reprimand, but the board voted to continue the school's accreditation.[8]

Meredith turned his grades around, but he was anything but euphoric at the end of the semester. His long struggle to gain admission and the harsh environment he encountered as a student had taken their toll on him, and he wondered if he could continue. He certainly did not second-guess his decision to attend Ole Miss. Some had suggested that he would have been better off somewhere where he could have gotten a better education and would not have had to endure the open hatred he faced in Oxford. He clung to his belief that if Mississippi blacks were to advance, they needed to be educated in the state at the same school that produced most of the state's lawyers and government leaders. "Harvard might teach you better that two and two are four," he wrote shortly after the semester ended, "but Harvard cannot teach you better how to use two and two is four in Mississippi." Moreover, because of his experiences and observations at Ole Miss, Meredith was more convinced than ever that only access to the university would enable deserving blacks to become professionals in Mississippi's legal, medical, business, and military life. As a veteran, he frequently watched the ROTC units drilling on Thursday afternoons on a parade ground located near Baxter Hall. He could not help but reflect on the absence of any blacks in the corps. "I know that not one Negro in Mississippi has the privilege of taking part in the ROTC program," he wrote. He thought that surely there were black students who were "officer material," and if they were denied the opportunity to seek a commission, the country would be a loser as well.[9]

By the end of the semester, Meredith decided that he would not register for classes for the spring semester. He made clear that he intended to remain at Ole Miss and finish the requirements for his degree, but he decided that he could not continue under the "present circumstances." He saw himself as a soldier engaged on the frontlines of a war against a "determined, resourceful, and unprincipled" enemy, and the enemy had thrown all it had against him for two years.

Meredith was beaten down and struggled to find the strength and courage to endure.

Meredith also regretted what his presence had done to the white students at Ole Miss. He had often expressed his sorrow over the loss of lives and the many injuries sustained on the night of rioting. He also feared that he had become a distraction for all students and faculty. "The thing that grieves me most about all this," he wrote in the November 10, 1962, issue of *Saturday Evening Post*, "is that the students are not getting the best college results because they're spending too much time looking at these various events involving me." Meredith's reflection might have been shortsighted. While his presence was a distraction, it also was a catalyst for opening the minds of many students, who theretofore had seldom reflected in a critical way on the Mississippi way of doing things.

Meredith lived in virtual isolation at Ole Miss. In his *Look* article in the spring of 1963, he declared, "Most of the time, I am perhaps the most segregated Negro in the world." Few who followed his year at Ole Miss would argue with that claim. However, in a sense the white students at Ole Miss were also isolated, and, ironically, Meredith's presence contributed to the breakdown of that isolation.

Fortunately for one attempting to gauge the outlook of Ole Miss students of 1962–1963, a survey of attitudes conducted just two years earlier provides valuable clues. Responses to the survey help answer the disturbing question of why so many students could have taken part in the rioting that led to the loss of life and how so many more could remain passive throughout the ordeal. In 1960–1961, a cross section of undergraduates in the university's five schools, the law school, and the graduate school completed a questionnaire called the College Characteristic Index. Devised by Professor C. Robert Pace of UCLA, the instrument was administered at 80 colleges and universities across the country. Its purpose was "to draw a picture of an educational institution as seen by its students, and ultimately, to study what happens when the student is, by temperament and outlook, at odds with his environment." The results of the survey were released for the first time in October 1962, just after the Ole Miss riot. Professor Pace reported that, compared to students elsewhere, Ole Miss students placed a high value on status and the material benefits of a college education—not a surprising attitude given Mississippi's low per capita income. Although Ole Miss students ranked above average in results of college entrance exams, the index showed that they had "little interest in scholarly pursuits or academic discipline once they arrived on campus." But the lowest ranking of Ole Miss students was in the category "esthetic sensitivity, idealism, involvement in the world's problems and self analysis."[10]

The finding of particular significance in the postriot climate of 1962 was the conclusion that Ole Miss students displayed a limited range of social and political opinion. Faculty interviewed for their reactions to the report generally agreed with its conclusions. To an "almost incredible" number, faculty members believed that "most of the students are uninformed and little interested in events and opinions in the rest of the nation and the world." In that regard, they agreed with history professor James Silver's characterization of Mississippi as a "closed society," where citizens not only showed little awareness of a larger world, but exhibited open hostility to "outside" opinions, especially those that were at odds with racial segregation, white supremacy, and states' rights. The professors added, however, that the admission and presence of James Meredith held the potential of prompting student engagement of social and political ideas and for sparking real debate over issues long regarded as settled. In the short run, they conceded, students were likely to retreat and become ever more isolated, but in time, the professors hoped, "Mr. Meredith may do more than anyone to start the processes of change working in the thought patterns of his classmates." Indeed, some faculty members thought that Meredith's presence was already "forcing the white students to think seriously for the first time about the racial issue and their attitudes toward it."[11] So, despite Meredith's worry that he was a distraction for serious study, there were indications of just the opposite: serious discussion that would challenge the closed society by vigorously debating a range of views about race relations.

Meredith's presence, the state's opposition to his admission, and the federal government's support of it sparked lively debate within and between the three most prominent student publications. The student newspaper, *The Mississippian*, voiced a moderate perspective and expressed a "spirit of accommodation" regarding integration of Ole Miss. At the opposite end of the spectrum was a subterranean newsletter that emerged during the Meredith crisis, *The Rebel Underground*, which reflected the extremist segregationist views of the Citizens' Councils. And, the school yearbook, *Ole Miss*, attempted to erase all memories of the riots by treating James Meredith as if he never existed and portraying the white students as soldiering on with courage and dignity.

Something of a print war broke out on campus in early 1962 as the editors of the *Mississippian* and those of the *Rebel Underground* expressed opposing views as to whether Meredith should be admitted to the university. The editor of the *Mississippian* was James Robertson of Greenville, whose editorials sympathetic to Meredith and hostile to Barnett and the Sovereignty Commission drew fire from segregationists both on the campus and throughout the state. After writing a piece entitled, "Sovereignty Commission Violates Bill of Rights," Robertson faced withering attacks from a new source, the *Rebel Underground*. A mimeographed newsletter that was barely legible, the pro-segregation paper enjoyed the support of the Citizens' Council and such right-wing commentators as columnist Tom Ethridge of the *Jackson Daily News*. The *Underground* called on the university senate to reprimand Robertson for his "extreme left-wing" writings, claiming that the *Mississippian* was "spieling the same liberal tripe as emanates from such magazines as EBONY [and] NEW REPUBLIC." Then in what sounded like a defiant call from the Council or the Klan, the *Underground* issued a call to arms: "if you value your racial heritage, if you have even the smallest regard for the future of this South of ours—you will be for segregation one hundred per cent. We must lock shields. We must fight for our race and for the South to the last bitter ditch."[12]

Robertson responded with a sympathetic front-page profile of James Meredith. He characterized Meredith as "a quiet student with few outside interests" and his wife Mary June as an "honor student and a brilliant girl." Robertson quoted from the Kosciusko newspaper, saying that the "Merediths are all good, solid, substantial citizens." And he concluded the article by defending Meredith's reasons for seeking admission to Ole Miss. "Meredith insists he would like to enroll at Ole Miss," Robertson wrote, "because Jackson State is an 'inferior school' and his educational opportunities would be greatly advanced at the state university." The editors of the *Rebel Underground* fired back that the *Mississippian's* favorable publicity for Meredith was nothing more than "an obvious attempt to plant into the mind of the student that Meredith is just a quiet timid young Negro, similar to our janitors."[13]

Robertson's successor as editor of the *Mississippian* for the 1962–1963 academic year was Sidna Brower, a senior from Memphis who grew up in the same segregated world as did her classmates, yet had never seen firsthand the kind of discrimination that the Meredith case exposed. Her editorials expressed her conviction that the university should be a place of accommodation, compromise, and order, and she was appalled by what she considered to be the seizure of Ole Miss by Ross Barnett and extremists who turned it into a violent battleground. Her first editorial following the riot set the tone for her commentary throughout the year. "Students started out yesterday by shouting slogans of pride in Mississippi," she wrote, "and ended up with nothing to be proud of. Last night the restraint and simple boisterousness that had marked most of the demonstrations in the Meredith situation degenerated into unrestrained hatred and violence." She reminded her fellow students that the Civil War was over and that there was no place for armed resistance to duly constituted government. "Whatever your beliefs," she asserted, "you are a citizen of the United States of America and of the State of Mississippi and should preserve the harmony of both governments." In the ensuing days as small groups of students demonstrated against Meredith's presence, sometimes accompanied by the destruction of property, Brower chided the administration for failing to maintain order. "It is disgusting to see such demonstrations permitted, especially when the rules are supposedly enforced," she wrote. She was offended that the same administration that took harsh action against students instigating "panty raids" should ignore much more serious assaults against those protecting Meredith. She asked, "Why should students be suspended for yelling 'We want panties' when they are allowed to throw rocks and yell profane and obscene comments at members of the United States Army?"[14]

The *Rebel Underground* responded by stepping up its attacks on Meredith. Its editors called on students across the campus to organize anti-Meredith groups in dormitories and fraternity and sorority houses. "Our primary objective," they wrote, "is to encourage James Meredith to transfer to some college where he would be welcome." In language that grew ever more racist, they suggested that "there are many Yankee colleges which would eulogize him and make him 'Tar

Baby' of the campus." The newsletter also attacked those who were sympathetic to Meredith, especially political science professor Russell Barrett, who on occasion ate breakfast with Meredith. The *Underground* called the professor a Communist and an "honorary nigger," and it referred to the federal marshals as the "KKK—Kennedy's Koon Keepers." Undaunted, Barrett continued to meet Meredith for coffee, and on one occasion he wore his World War II ribbons on his lapel along with the "honorary nigger" card that the *Underground* had sent him.[15]

Brower's editorials calling for campus peace and reconciliation attracted the attention of national journalists and gained her notoriety. One of her pieces was reprinted in the *New York Times*, inspiring hundreds of readers to send her letters, some of which she placed in the *Mississippian*. Some students, including the editors of the *Rebel Underground*, charged her with a liberal bias evident in her printing more letters sympathetic to her views than critical of them. She defended her policy by pointing out that she did indeed include unfavorable comments, such as those of one letter writer who compared her to the infamous Tokyo Rose of World War II. She also explained that most of the critical letters were filled with obscenities and profanity and were unsigned, thus violating paper policies. Nonetheless, her detractors filed charges against her in the student senate. Led by George Monroe, a leader of the Patriotic American Youth, a "kind of college-aged Citizens' Council," the opposition drafted a resolution censuring Brower and making clear that the senate did not agree with her editorial position. In particular, Monroe and his supporters were outraged over Brower's failure to condemn the federal marshals for violating white students' civil rights. After 10 days of debate, the senate passed a compromise resolution, not censuring the editor, but reprimanding her, a distinction that would be lost in the reporting. Indeed, the *New York Times* headlined its account of the episode with, "Mississippi Student Group Denounces Editor." The Ole Miss faculty joined the dispute, passing a resolution of their own commending Brower for her "unwavering determination to follow a constructive editorial policy."[16]

Regardless of which side they supported, students across the campus were engaging in a serious debate over civil rights, freedom of the press, race relations, and states' rights. While Meredith's presence caused some disturbance in student events—such as forcing the homecoming football game against the University of Houston to be transferred to Jackson—it also provoked students to rethink many of their most cherished assumptions, such as segregation as the best plan for race relations, states' rights as justification for violating federal law, and elected state officials as honorable promoters of justice.

Certainly not all students were politicized by campus debates over Meredith's presence. Many wished to ignore him and all that swirled about him and cling to the university's and the state's time-honored traditions. That was the sentiment expressed in the 1963 edition of the university's yearbook, *Ole Miss*. For the editors, the academic year was one to be remembered for the expression of Mississippi traditions during a time of great hardship. And the heroes in this nostalgic reflection were the white students and their leaders. Ross Barnett was hailed as a "devoted and illustrious alumnus of the University of Mississippi," who confronted with grace and courage "the most trying difficulties that could be put upon a governor and a state." The *Ole Miss* trumpeted triumphantly that "our governor has brought the state through these trying times with a dignified perseverance." The book was organized in sections that viewed events of 1962 against the historical backdrop of a century earlier. The section featuring campus beauties, usually devoid of any political reference, depicted the student body at war and carried powerful images of a defiant and proud South. The photographs of the contestants for the most beautiful woman were taken at the military park in Vicksburg, and one picture showed the finalists posing in front of an artillery piece. In the section featuring fraternities, the rebel flag was draped on the front with a placard beneath that says, "Cuba, U.S. Steel, Ole Miss, What Next?" in a reference to the Kennedy Administration's "invasions." The last section of the yearbook, entitled "The Reconstruction," conjured images of the last time federal troops occupied the state of Mississippi. Under the masthead, "Way down yonder, in the land of cotton," was a photograph of a soldier in full combat gear complete with his M1 rifle, with the caption, "U.S. 1, Mississippi 0." Another photo on the same page showed the rear end of a U.S. Army truck driving away from the camera with the caption, "Yankee Go Home!" On the next page was a picture of a student showing his student identification card to a marshal while wearing a tag that said, "Made in Occupied

Mississippi." A shot of the campus at night carried the caption, "Midnight in Moscow."[17]

The *Ole Miss* was dedicated to the students of the university, meaning the white students, for their "unfaltering trust" in the institution during its severest test. Because of those students' resolve and courage, the editors proclaimed, the "opportunity for an education still exists." The meaning is clear; the words "still exists" means still exists for white students, as if nothing had changed. Not a word about James Meredith's incredible courage in braving the intense opposition to his admission and presence. Not a word about the opportunity that his actions gave *all* Mississippians. Not a word about the historic significance of events at Ole Miss in 1962. And not a word about how those events shattered the claims of extremists that Mississippi would forever be a bastion of segregation and white supremacy. To portray their fiction of Ole Miss-the-same, the yearbook editors removed Meredith from the book. There is no mention of his name, no photograph alongside those of his classmates, no reference whatever. He was erased from the history in which he played the central role.

When viewed from a distance of more than 45 years, such attitudes as those found in the *Ole Miss* seem difficult to fathom. How could college students be more concerned about the images of a vanished age than the historic events that occurred on their own campus that year? We want an explanation for the actions and attitudes of the white students at Ole Miss, especially the vast majority that never threatened or taunted Meredith but also never showed him the slightest human kindness.

Just as white students wanted to ignore Meredith and get on with their educations, Meredith wished to be a "normal" student, that is, one whose every move did not attract attention. At the beginning of the second semester he commented that "no student should be subjected to the fanfare" that he endured the first semester. After much deliberation and conversation with his wife, he decided to return to Ole Miss for the spring semester with a goal of graduating in August. He had transferred enough credits to make that possible provided that he took a full load and maintained an adequate grade point average. After receiving the mid-term warning in November, he had improved his grades appreciably, primarily by eliminating as many distractions as he could—for instance, he put off the book deal—and focusing on his course work. The spring and summer semesters went much more smoothly. He had settled into a disciplined routine of studying; his grades improved; and he began to think that his dream of graduating would soon become a reality.

In spring 1963, Meredith for the first time engaged his fellow students on the question of his admission and presence at Ole Miss. On May 3, 1963, Meredith published an open letter to the student body in an attempt to offer a rational explanation for what he was attempting to do. In the letter published in the *Mississippian*, he stated once more that he had chosen Ole Miss for the same reason that they had; it offered the best educational opportunity in the state. He contended that he had "little concern for the phenomenon of integration and desegregation. Neither is my aim." To make his point more clear on a campus with a robust Greek system, he added, "I don't want to join your fraternities." He then asked questions of the white students: "What is everybody so mad about? I know of nothing that I have done to offend anyone." Second, he asked, "do you feel that Negro students are just as entitled to having the opportunity of becoming a doctor, lawyer, engineer, accountant, or an officer in the military, as the white student?"[18]

Reaction to the letter was mixed, another indication that student opinion was divided over Meredith's presence and purpose. One student viewed Meredith's desegregation of Ole Miss as important not only for the university but for the state, arguing that if Mississippi was to become wealthy and productive, it must make Negroes full citizens. Only then could the state gain maximum benefit from the 43 percent of its citizens who happened to be black, and only then would it attract outside capital. New investment would more likely come if there were a better educated workforce and an improved education system so that executives could be assured that their children would receive a first-rate education. But others could not get beyond race. Responding to Meredith, one student defiantly stated: you are no "fellow student." The letter also referred to unspecified "contemptuous acts," foremost of which was Meredith's audacity to seek admission in the first place. The letter writer asserted that Mississippi "spends much more on the Negroes in education than it does on whites." Although state budget figures did not bear out that claim, the implication was that Mississippi had good Negro schools, and Meredith should have stayed in his place and attended one of them.[19]

On August 18, 1963, James Meredith graduated from Ole Miss. It was a momentous occasion for him, the university, and the state. For Meredith, it was also an occasion for personal reflection. He recalled that as a boy in Kosciusko he had set three goals for himself: "to become an 'unadjectived' man; to run for governor of Mississippi and get all the Negroes' votes; and to get a degree from the University of Mississippi." His painful experiences over the past two and a half years had reminded him that Mississippi was nowhere near ready to regard a black person as an "unadjectived" person; he had always been identified in racial terms, such as Negro or black or colored student, as well as the more racist epithets hurled at him. But, he had attained the third goal. And he knew that earning a degree from Ole Miss had required far more of him than it had of the other graduates. His degree had been "impossible to achieve...without seriously disrupting and undermining the system of 'White Supremacy.'" And, with satisfaction, he realized that "although the system had not been broken by my receiving a degree from the university, it had surely been disrupted." Yet, it was now clear to him that a degree from Ole Miss was insufficient for a run for governor because "the Negro has no effective vote in Mississippi." He knew that what he had accomplished, though important for Mississippi's civil rights movement, was only one step in many that must be taken to secure equal rights and opportunity. And his experience at Ole Miss taught him that future steps would require great courage, perseverance, and sacrifice from black Mississippians as well as support from the federal government.

On graduation day, Meredith braced himself for insulting comments and taunts, something with which he had grown accustomed, but he did not want his 72-year-old father and 3-year-old son to be subjected to such rude behavior. To his surprise, none was forthcoming. His "marching mate" in the processional offered no resistance to her role, nor did any of his fellow graduates show resentment to his presence. Further, he heard no "unpleasant remarks" from students

James Meredith graduates from Ole Miss.
"Mississippi Gives Meredith Degree," New York Times, 8/19/1963, p.1

"All the News That's Fit to Print"

The New York Times.

LATE CITY EDITION
U.S. Weather Bureau Report (see details): Sunny today; partly cloudy tonight. Cloudy tomorrow.
Temp. range: 80—60; yesterday: 77—63.
Temp.-Hum. Index: 73—70; yesterday: 70.

VOL. CXII—No. 38,558.

NEW YORK, MONDAY, AUGUST 19, 1963.

TEN CENTS

HOUSE PREPARES FOR ANNUAL FIGHT OVER FOREIGN AID

Administration Aim in Battle Starting Tomorrow Is to Hold Line at 4.1 Billion

BUDGET DEFICIT FACTOR

Senators to Continue Study of Test Ban Treaty With Joint Chiefs' Testimony

By FELIX BELAIR Jr.
Special to The New York Times

TURKEY ROUNDS UP 'LEFTIST' LEADERS AFTER COUP TRIAL

Regime Indicates Arrests Total 20, but Others Put Figure as High as 200

By FRED POWLEDGE

New Rebel Invasion Is Charged by Haiti

By HENRY RAYMONT

ALLIANCE DRAFTS WIDER LATIN ROLE IN CHANNELING AID

New Board to Set Priorities for Development Projects and Enforce Reforms

U.S. RETAINS FUND REIN

By TAD SZULC

GRADUATION DAY: James H. Meredith receives diploma from Chancellor J. D. Williams at University of Mississippi

ROCKEFELLER URGES 'MINIMUM BUDGET'

Says National Growth Rate Lag Forces State to Pare Spending in 1964-'65

CORE Expects Agreement On Jobs Here in 2 Weeks

MISSISSIPPI GIVES MEREDITH DEGREE

He Is First Negro Graduate of University—440 Whites Also Receive Diplomas

POPE RENEWS BID TO ORTHODOX RITE

COURTS TO SPEED COUNCIL DECISION

41 HURT BY BLAST IN BRUSSELS CAFE

BIG 3 WILL TAKE ATOM-PACT TO U.N.

Thousands of Buddhists Rally at Saigon Pagoda

The Off-Track Betting Question: How the Systems Work Abroad

Continued on Page (various)

in attendance. He did, however, have painful memories of his admission. As the students passed the Lyceum Building, he noted that bullet holes were still visible. He also passed within sight of the statue of the Confederate soldier, to him a symbol of the fight for "white supremacy" waged, first, 100 years earlier and, second, 18 months ago. He was pleased to see as he entered the Grove, traditionally an all-white ground for elegant tailgate parties, a "large number" of black people gathered to witness his graduation. The ceremony went off without incident, and Meredith received his diploma from Chancellor Williams, who shook his hand and offered some congratulatory remarks. Meredith was particularly pleased that his father could see him graduate and, more importantly, see the day when Mississippi would be open to his grandchildren and their children. As Meredith reflected on the historic occasion of his graduation, he wrote, "This was the first time in the history of the state that a Negro had ever been enrolled in a school which Mississippi had reserved for its privileged whites." His father was more impressed with the moment, observing that white people, at whose hands he had seen his share of meanness and contempt, "can be decent."[20]

Newspapers from around the country covered Meredith's graduation. The August 19 edition of the *New York Times* carried a banner headline: *Mississippi Gives Meredith Degree*. Noting the historical significance of the occasion, the article reminded readers that Meredith was the "first Negro Graduate" in the 115-year history of Ole Miss, and thus becomes the "first Negro Alumnus." The writer observed that Meredith received his diploma just 100 yards from the scene of the "bloody riots that accompanied his admission last September 30." The reporter noted that the ceremony itself opened with a message of hope expressed in the invocation by Rev. William Arthur Pennington of the St. Andrews Methodist Church of Oxford that, out of the difficult times surrounding Meredith's days at Ole Miss, there will be "unity out of discord, love out of hate, and hope out of despair." The commencement speaker, Dr. John A. Hunter, President of Louisiana State University (LSU), emphasized the achievements of Ole Miss and its administration more than the courage of James Meredith. "For many years," he told the audience, "the university and LSU have engaged a traditional rivalry on the gridiron,... but let this not obscure the fact that your traditional athletic rivals have been intensely sympathetic toward you in your time of crisis." He ended by applauding Ole Miss for maintaining its "academic tradition" under the trying circumstances.

Some newspapers highlighted the historic significance of the graduation by examining its interracial character. The *Times-Record* of Troy, New York, noted that white people sat on either side of Meredith's family during the ceremony held in the Grove. The *Hammond-Times* reported that "the white people stared stiffly ahead without expression," while the "few Negroes in the audience watched somberly in small, self-conscious groups." The *Albuquerque Tribune* captured the unprecedented character of the gathering in speaking of both whites and blacks: "Together, under the tall oaks, they sat in awkward silence and watched what neither had ever seen before."

Other newspapers, especially in the South, Southwest, and border states, offered less sympathetic accounts. Several referred to Meredith's degree as the "5-Million Dollar Diploma," alluding to the estimated federal government expenditure to support his admission. Some articles included sentiments expressed by white Mississippians attending the ceremony. One matronly white woman whispered in dismay to a friend when Meredith approached Chancellor Williams to receive his diploma, "Oh, look, he's going to shake his hand." After the ceremony, two white women exchanged their views of the event in the following conversation:

"Well, I'm glad he's gone."
"There'll be others."
"Well, let's hope it'll all be quieter."

Writing 30 years later, historian David Sansing provided historical perspective for Meredith's graduation. His succinct assessment of the change that Meredith's graduation triggered is expansive: "Before James Meredith enrolled at Ole Miss, no other public school in Mississippi—grammar school, or college—had been integrated. Everything was segregated: public parks, playgrounds, libraries, beaches, theaters, doctors' offices, lunch counters, cafes, water fountains, hospitals, motels, and even cemeteries. But the color line was now broken."[21] The claim that the color line was "broken" by Meredith appears to be a bit optimistic, certainly where Ole Miss was concerned. Big questions loomed after August 1963. What about the next African American student to attend Ole Miss? Would he or she be able to walk freely around campus and enjoy the experience of being a student without the presence of armed soldiers? On the one hand, Meredith's individual courage had changed much. It was an outstanding example of bravery and a reminder that the civil rights movement was about aggregate individual and collective acts of heroism. On the other hand, Mississippi's racial attitudes remained strong even after the important battle of Ole Miss, and, indeed, new versions of white supremacy emerged. The next black students at Ole Miss would be inspired by Meredith's courage while being challenged by determined resistance.

....

CHAPTER 8

Intended and Unintended Consequences

....

Mississippi is a much better state today because of James
Meredith, and this is a much better university.

Morgan Freeman, 2006

....

Forty-five years after the Battle of Ole Miss, the battleground has
an altered appearance. In a fitting tribute to James Meredith's
fight for admission, the university in 2006 under the leadership
of Chancellor Robert Khayat dedicated a life-size bronze statue of
Meredith. Mounted atop a 17-foot-tall limestone pedestal, the monument stands just the length of a football field from the Confederate
Statue, the rallying point for so many who tried to prevent Meredith's
enrollment. Appropriately, the new statue sums up in four words what
Meredith sought in 1961 and what his actions represent: courage,
perseverance, opportunity, and knowledge. In remarks at the dedication ceremony, actor Morgan Freeman from nearby Clarksdale linked
the fortunes of Meredith with those of the state and the university:
"Mississippi is a much better state today because of James Meredith,
and this is a much better university." Freeman added, "Thank you,
Mr. Meredith."[1]

While James Meredith attended the ceremony, he did not speak.
He had prepared a speech for the occasion, but organizers who read
his manuscript thought his comments were too dark and political for
the celebratory event they envisioned. So Meredith remained silent.
In the text that he had prepared, he saw his efforts in 1962 in military

Meredith monument near the Lyceum Building.
From the collection of Joseph Allenus

terms, as the first battle in a war. He wrote, "My objective in this war was total victory: victory over discrimination, oppression, the unequal application of the law, and, most of all, over White Supremacy and all of its manifestations." He thought that the war was far from over, even at Ole Miss, where thousands of African Americans had earned degrees. Racial equality remained elusive, he wrote, and the most obvious indication was the hyphenated nature of black life on campus: Black-Student Union, Black-History, Black-Alumni Association. White Supremacy and its opposite "Black Inferiority" would continue at Ole Miss, he thought, until such time as all students were regarded and treated in every way as simply Ole Miss students. So to James Meredith, the monument in his honor was more a reminder of what needed to be done than a memorial to what he had accomplished in 1962.[2]

Though Meredith failed to achieve "total victory" in 1962, nonetheless, his actions made a significant and lasting impact on Ole Miss as well as on the State of Mississippi and the South. The most direct and profound influence was seen at the University of Mississippi. At the time of the unveiling ceremony in 2006, African Americans constituted 11 percent of the student body and about 20 percent of the faculty and staff. After Meredith's pioneering effort, black students across Mississippi who had dreams similar to those of the 14-year-old James Meredith now had more realistic expectations of seeing them come true. They had a better chance of getting the best education the state had to offer and, with it, the opportunity for a better life. But Meredith's accomplishment should not be overstated. What he did at Ole Miss was an important milestone in the fight for civil rights in Mississippi, but it was but one moment in a larger struggle. While Meredith operated in the glare of national and international media attention, and thus became the best known figure in black Mississippians' fight for justice, hundreds of other students risked their lives in equally courageous efforts to desegregate public facilities, break down employment discrimination, and register African American voters.

Meredith's admission to Ole Miss was far from the first event in an unbroken chain of victories, nor did it represent a linear progression in the transformation of race relations in Mississippi. Rather, the fight for civil rights in Mississippi proceeded in fits and starts, as had been tragically illustrated on the eve of Meredith's graduation. As Medgar Evers returned home from an NAACP meeting shortly after midnight on June 12, 1963, he was shot in the back of his head by an assassin, later identified as Byron de la Beckwith, a member of the Citizens' Council and the KKK. Speaking at the funeral, Meredith called Evers "one of my best and most beloved friends" and vowed to carry on the fight "at any cost."[3] He knew that the fight would be difficult for him and for those who came after him.

The first three black students to follow Meredith at Ole Miss best represented the newly won hope for Mississippi blacks—hope tempered by the reality that race hatred continued to run deeply in the state. Cleve McDowell, a 21-year-old graduate from Jackson State entered Ole Miss Law School in early June 1963. Though the university had fought his admission and he had to file a lawsuit to gain entrance, McDowell started classes in a calm atmosphere, a sharp contrast to that of September 1962. Rooming with Meredith, McDowell had a valuable ally, one, moreover, who had federal protection. After attending summer classes without serious incident, McDowell got off to a smooth start for fall semester 1963 on a calm campus that was nothing like that of a year earlier. However, there were no federal marshals protecting him because both university administrators and Justice Department officials believed that their presence was disruptive and their removal would reduce tensions. McDowell was concerned about the lack of protection, especially when he drove the car he had purchased from Meredith, a car well known to segregationists. But, he went to classes without incident in the early days of the semester. To be sure, he heard taunts and jeers as he walked across the campus, and he lived alone in Meredith's old room. In fact, no one else lived on his floor in Baxter Hall; all the white students moved away, refusing to live in proximity to a Negro.

McDowell's family supported their son's decision to attend Ole Miss, and they paid dearly for that support. Because they lived in the middle of the black community of Drew, Mississippi, a small Delta town located about 80 miles southwest of Oxford, they were protected from physical violence. However, they faced economic sanctions as local stores where they had shopped for years cut off their credit. Further, when Cleve drove to Drew, he was on at least one occasion forced off the road and on others had rocks and gravel thrown at his car. So, in a move understandable for a young, black student at Ole Miss without federal protection, McDowell decided to protect himself by purchasing a gun to carry in his car. Even though he knew that guns were prohibited on campus—like other students he had signed a card stating that he would abide by the regulation—he felt more secure with it. On Monday, September 23 he was late for class, ironically because he had stopped at the U.S. Attorney's office in Oxford to ask for federal protection, and parked in a no-parking zone. Because he thought he might get a ticket, he took his handgun with him, but as he ran upstairs to his class, the gun fell out of his jacket pocket and clattered onto the floor. Two law students who saw the incident called the Lafayette County sheriff, who arrested McDowell when he emerged from class. He was immediately suspended from the university, and the next day he was expelled after the student judicial council recommended that he be removed. Once again, Ole Miss was an all-white institution.[4]

Nonetheless, other courageous young blacks dared to follow Meredith's pioneering journey as Ole Miss students. First there were lone individuals who, despite Cleve McDowell's expulsion and despite the virulent anti–civil rights resistance across the state, were determined to enter the university. Cleveland Donald, Jr., an 18-year-old transfer student from Tougaloo College, became the third black admitted and the second to graduate. Like McDowell, he had had to go to court and obtain an order to gain admission, and also like McDowell, he had no federal protection while a student at Ole Miss. Despite insults and harassment from a small minority of white students, Donald became the second black graduate. A year after Donald enrolled, in fall 1964, Irwin Walker became the first black student to be admitted to Ole Miss without having to seek a court order. Walker tried his best to fit into student life, participating in freshmen activities along with his classmates. To be sure, there were some students who refused to speak to him and others who tried to intimidate him by such antics as hanging a funeral wreath on his dormitory door. But, most students had at least determined that an integrated university was a reality and that all students must find a way to get along. That Ole Miss was not yet integrated was made painfully clear to the first African American students who enrolled but were hardly part of the university's fabric and identity. But there was hope that things would change. One incident illustrating that interracial peace could be attained came, ironically, when Walker and a white student who had insulted him got into a brief fight. Rather than the fracas escalating into a race riot, it ended peacefully, and the *Mississippian*'s coverage of the incident was low-key and aimed at promoting goodwill.

To understand the resistance that the first four black students at Ole Miss faced, one must consider that their efforts were but part of determined efforts by blacks across Mississippi to win their civil rights—efforts that were met by equally determined opposition led by the Citizens' Council. A group of Tougaloo College students organized a boycott of Jackson retailers. The boycotters had four basic demands of the merchants: equal opportunity in hiring and promotion; desegregated restrooms, water fountains, and lunch counters; courtesy titles of "Mr." and "Mrs." extended to Negros; and service on a first-come, first-served basis. On May 28, 1963, three Tougaloo students, Anne

Moody, Memphis Norman, and Pearlena Lewis, entered the Woolworth store on Capitol Street in Jackson and sat at the white section of the lunch counter. Soon a crowd of whites appeared, taunting them, pouring catsup, mustard, and soda on them, and finally beating them to the floor. All the while, members of the Jackson Police Department, who had been alerted to the sit-in, stood outside and offered no assistance to the students.[5] While most blacks supported the boycott, the Citizens' Council waged its own retaliatory program, threatening to foreclose the mortgages of boycotters and waging a white boycott against merchants that met the blacks' demands.

Another civil rights initiative that increased racial tensions in the early 1960s was a massive voter registration drive. Led by Mississippi black activists, especially college students, and assisted by such organizations as SNCC and the Council of Federated Organizations (COFO), civil rights workers undertook the brave but daunting task of registering blacks in a state that systematically kept blacks from voting through such legal means as white primaries, poll taxes, and competency tests and extralegal tactics of intimidation and violence. In its customary patronizing tone, the Citizens' Council along with most newspapers portrayed voter registration as coming from outside invaders, not from Mississippi blacks, most of whom, they argued, were content with the Mississippi way of doing things. Although it understated the roles of African American students in Mississippi, the Council was not completely wrong in its perspective that a growing number of outsiders were fomenting racial activism.

In the summer of 1964, as Irwin Walker prepared to enter Ole Miss, three civil rights workers were murdered in a voter registration drive in Philadelphia, Mississippi. James Chaney, a 21-year-old black man from nearby Meridian and two whites from New York, Andrew Goodman and Michael Schwerner, were driven off the road, shot to death, and buried in an earthen dam near the town located about 150 miles south-southeast of Oxford. The case attracted national publicity and an army of federal investigators. The Justice Department eventually charged 18 men with violating the three men's civil rights. Indicative of the systemic nature of race hatred and anti-segregation sentiments, the sheriff, deputy sheriff, and a local minister were included in those charged. More than three years after the murders, seven men were found guilty of violating the three victims' civil rights.

The Philadelphia murders underscored both the courage and the challenges faced by Irwin Walker and the blacks who followed him at Ole Miss. They attended classes without any federal protection on an open campus in a state seething with animosity toward blacks in general, but in particular toward blacks who were at the forefront of efforts to desegregate. As had been demonstrated in 1962, even when the campus was ringed by state and federal officials, extremists had no difficulty gaining access to the campus. But Walker prevailed and graduated.

After Walker's admission, the path to Ole Miss widened for Mississippi blacks, and black students began to arrive in numbers. For the summer session of 1966, just four years after Meredith's admission, more than 30 blacks registered for classes. What was noteworthy is that their admission was not newsworthy, or at least did not attract the coverage that had attended the arrival of earlier black students. The June 16 edition of the *Mississippian* reported that "the registration attracted no attention,...a marked contrast to the events occurring when James Meredith broke the color barrier here in 1962." The reference to Meredith underscored the historic significance of his path-breaking feat.

As more black students entered Ole Miss, they not only found greater security in numbers, but they also began to address issues that pertained specifically to blacks. One group of students, who referred to themselves simply as "Several Black Students," sent a memo to Chancellor Porter Fortune (Chancellor Williams had recently retired) entitled, "Bigotry, Bias and Racial Prejudice." This was a signal of a new day at Ole Miss. If white students before 1962 by and large ignored political debate, especially that pertaining to race and segregation, black students now made that debate the centerpiece of their demands. In bold terms they declared that "there prevails an atmosphere of bigotry, bias, and prejudice because the faculty, staff, administration, diverse officers, officials, teachers and workers facilitate and substantiate said atmosphere." Like Rev. Duncan Gray and other whites who acknowledged that it was white leaders in schools, churches, and government that had created a culture of racial bigotry, these black students blamed the university's leadership, not the students, with the prevailing climate of prejudice and hatred. The students asked that they be allowed to create a Black Student Union on campus that would enjoy the same recognition, rights, and privileges as other student organizations. And, recognizing that history as taught in Mississippi had excluded favorable accounts of black people and their contributions, the students asked that Negro History Week be observed at Ole Miss as it had been for more than 40 years at many other colleges and universities around the country. Fortune granted the second request, and the first Negro History Week in Ole Miss history was celebrated in February 1969. Visiting professors from other universities delivered lectures on "Black Identity" and "Development and Trends in Black Thought." In addition, the library featured a black history display and the Fine Arts Center a display of black art.[6] While black students recognized such efforts as an important first step, they were far from satisfied and stepped up their pressure on the administration to address their broader list of concerns and grievances.

The conversation about race and civil rights that Meredith began at Ole Miss produced small but vocal groups of activists on campus. Some were all African American, some all white, and some integrated. But what they all had in common was a determination to find and express their own views about issues that for too long in Mississippi had been formed by an older generation with the expectation that their children and grandchildren would accept those views uncritically. Activists were determined to think for themselves, to try to understand why race relations and attitudes were the way they were, why civil rights had been systematically denied to African Americans, and why Mississippi leaders had been allowed to perpetrate lies in the service of gross injustices. One group, the law student association, decided in 1966 to conduct its own investigation of the Ole Miss riot of 1962. Why had things been conducted so poorly? Why had politicians allowed events to run out of control? Ole Miss students to that point had heard only explanations from Mississippi leaders, explanations that blamed the federal government for the troubles. The law students wanted to broaden the investigation by examining how federal officials saw the event. Accordingly, they invited Robert Kennedy to speak at Ole Miss. The invitation in itself was a remarkable moment in the university's and the state's history. Here college students dared to invite a man, characterized by the *Mississippian* as "a man with a prominent name, radical views, high placed friends and powerful enemies—and nowhere are those enemies more numerous than in the state of Mississippi."[7] Such an invitation would have been out of the question before 1962.

Equally remarkable was the speech itself and its reception by the Ole Miss students. More than 5,000 students, faculty, and staff poured into the Coliseum to hear the speech on Friday afternoon, October 18. In a gracious and conciliatory address, Kennedy spoke about the need for greater understanding between North and South. He told the audience, "You have no problem the nation does not have. You share no hope that is not shared by your fellow students and young people across this country. You carry no burden that they too do not carry." Here the attorney general whose brother had sent federal troops onto the Ole Miss campus was embracing students and assuring them that no matter how Mississippi politicians had sought to build a closed society, they were all part of one nation. In the question-and-answer session that followed, Kennedy responded candidly to student questions about what had transpired in the days and hours leading up to the riot on September 30, 1962. He took them behind the scenes, and for the first time students learned about Barnett's overriding concerns about finding political cover when he agreed to admit Meredith after shouting "Never" for two years. Kennedy had the students roaring in laughter when he recounted how many marshals Barnett wanted to draw their guns before the governor retreated. While Barnett railed against Kennedy's speech, the reality certainly was not lost on him and other state politicians that it was a new day at Ole Miss.[8] Students would make their own judgments about what happened, and they would decide what sources were most credible.

By the late 1960s, African American students at Ole Miss were emboldened not only by their growing numbers on campus, but by the inspiration of a civil rights movement that had become more confident and militant in confronting race hatred and state-sponsored discrimination. While their parents had grown up in the 1930s, '40s, and '50s, when black activists were routinely intimidated and often killed, these students had new models of strong blacks who refused to back down even in the face of violence such as Medgar Evers' assassination and the murders at Philadelphia. Both outside and inside the state, blacks were standing up and demanding that the federal government protect their civil rights.

In 1966, James Meredith, who had already attained iconic status for black students entering Ole Miss, displayed unflinching courage in confronting racial bigotry as well as facing the fear that blacks felt every day. In June 1966, Meredith began his March Against Fear, a proposed walk from Memphis to Jackson for two purposes: one, to demonstrate to black Mississippians that they must overcome fear and act, and two, that they must register to vote as a first step in bringing down state-sponsored race discrimination. The march came in the midst of racial tension and violence in Mississippi and also at a time when the civil rights movement was shifting to a more militant level. From his first application to Ole Miss in December 1961 to his graduation in August 1963, James Meredith had been the epitome of courage, facing every setback with resolve, enduring every insult with equanimity, and persevering at great personal sacrifice to open doors that had been locked to African Americans for 115 years. During his ordeal, he had dealt with threats to his life, and he had repeatedly stated that he was unafraid to die. As a young boy he had learned from his father that death was preferable to the loss of dignity. Cap Meredith taught his children to never enter a white person's house through the back door as was the prevailing practice under Mississippi's white-dominated culture, a lesson etched in James' character. In his book, *Three Years in Mississippi*, published in the same year as his march, Meredith wrote, "I was taught to believe that the most dishonorable thing that a Meredith could do was to work in a white woman's kitchen and take care of a white man's child. I know that I would starve to death rather than do either." During his struggle to enter Ole Miss, he repeated his determination to fight for justice even if it meant death. Meredith admitted that he was afraid, as would have been any Mississippi African American who was aware of the fates of their brothers and sisters who had challenged white supremacy, but his fear was more that of doing nothing in the face of injustice than fearing death.[9]

So, fully aware of the dangers lurking along Highway 51, Meredith set out from Memphis on his March Against Fear. As he entered Mississippi on the second day, he was shot from ambush just outside Hernando, Mississippi. Fortunately his wounds were not life-threatening; they were inflicted by birdshot pellets intended to send a message, not to kill. So after a short stay in the hospital, Meredith was discharged. More significant for the civil rights movement in Mississippi, his one-man march was continued by high-profile national leaders, including Martin Luther King, and it contributed to a shift toward militancy.

Meredith's abortive march represented an act of courage. It also exposed a fundamental shift in the leadership and tactics of the civil rights movement. In May 1966, just before Meredith began his march, Stokely Carmichael, a brash, eloquent New Yorker, became chairman of the SNCC, replacing John Lewis, a religious Alabaman. Carmichael moved the organization in a much more militant direction, away from the Christian nonviolence preferred by Lewis and Martin Luther King. Carmichael was catapulted into the national spotlight following Meredith's being shot. He had joined the March Against Fear along with Rev. King, and when the march arrived in Greenwood he was arrested and put in jail, a stay that was to be a life-changing experience. When he was released, he addressed a large crowd in East Greenwood, the black section of town, and informed them that this was his twenty-seventh arrest and that he had run out of patience. It was time for a change in goals and tactics. "We been saying 'Freedom' for six years," he shouted. "What we are going to start saying now is 'Black Power.'"[10]

As the civil rights movement became bolder and more militant and as the number of students increased at Ole Miss, African Americans on campus grew more confident and assertive. Moreover, they had some allies among white students, namely the Ole Miss Young Democrats. In fact, the Young Democrats, the only student organization that was integrated, welcomed African American students. That reason alone would have made the group suspect in the eyes of most white Mississippians, but in 1968 the students were supportive of the "liberal" national Democratic ticket of Hubert Humphrey and Edmund Muskie. The Mississippi Democratic Party rejected both the national ticket and its platform as being out of sync with the party's populist history and out of tune with Mississippi sentiments and interests, especially those regarding race relations and states' rights. The Young Democrats thought that most Ole Miss students were too apathetic about political issues and were too willing to accept their parents' views on race relations without engaging in serious, independent reflection. One member, David Molpus, complained that most Ole Miss students were unwilling to rebel "against what their parents thought," a complaint that echoed the observations of a *New York*

Times reporter who characterized the university as "little more than a party school attended by emptyheaded offspring of planters and bankers." The Young Democrats wanted to shake the student body from its apathy, and they found a way to do that in the fall of 1968.[11]

In an unprecedented move, the Young Democrats invited one of the leading civil rights figures in the state to give a political speech on campus. Charles Evers had succeeded his brother Medgar as head of the NAACP, and upon the announcement by John Bell Williams, an arch-segregationist, that he would not seek re-election to the U.S. House of Representatives, Evers announced that he would run. He knew that white voters would be wary if not outright hostile to his campaign, and he knew that he had little chance of being elected. Nonetheless, he believed that it was important for blacks and whites alike to see a black man run for public office, and he took on the major issues of the day, including welfare. He agreed with many whites who thought that too many African Americans were on welfare. Evers advocated the notion of workfare, one of the first in the country to do so, arguing that everyone should work and contending that all could do something, even it were piecework, to earn a paycheck. In the Democratic Primary he ran against what he characterized as "six white racist candidates," and the electorate was split along race lines. Thus, he was pleased when the Ole Miss Young Democrats invited him to the campus to deliver a speech. That invitation would soon embroil the students in a political fight against the university, the state, and, in many cases, their parents.

Fearing dissent from white Mississippi orthodoxy on race, the Ole Miss administration and the Board of Trustees of Mississippi Institutions of Higher Learning followed a policy aimed at limiting free speech. While proclaiming deep regard for free speech in the abstract, their policy declared that the university had the right to block whomever it wished from speaking on campus, that free speech did not mean anyone could address any group on any subject. When the Young Democrats filed their request for Evers' speech, they soon learned firsthand the limitations of free speech at Ole Miss. Administration officials informed them that Evers could not speak because there had been insufficient time for the administration to get approval from the Board of Trustees, and, besides, Evers' speech would be "political" and therefore disallowed. Rather than accepting the decision, the Young

Democrats sued and the federal judge at Oxford ordered the administration to let Evers speak. What is remarkable about the event was not the speech, which went off without a hitch, but that an integrated group of students had taken a position opposed to that held by most white Mississippians and, despite opposition by the administration and the state, had prevailed in promoting real free speech. Such a step would have been unthinkable prior to Meredith's entrance. Evers saw the occasion as hopeful. He wrote of the event, "Young whites had begun seeing that their parents were wrong about race. The next generation aimed to do better."[12]

Ole Miss students continued to express ambivalence in their attitudes toward race. On the one hand, many were willing to see blacks as fellow students who should be judged by their character and achievements, not by the color of their skin. On the other hand, many whites were uneasy about interracial relationships and wished to maintain racial boundaries. The story of Ben Williams illustrates that ambivalence. In 1975 Ben Williams, an All-American football player, who in 1971 along with John Reed had become one of the first African Americans recruited for the football team, became the first African American to be elected "Colonel Rebel" (the title for "Mr. Ole Miss"), an ironic honor given the controversy surrounding the school's mascot, a figure that roamed the sidelines in Confederate garb also known as "Colonel Reb." To be sure, his election presented challenges to white sensibilities. How can a black man and a white woman be photographed together without confirming the segregationist fears of race-mixing and amalgamation? The editors handled it by posing the couple on either side of a white picket fence that, they thought, provided a proper boundary.

Ben Williams was a talented football player, but he proved to be the exception. Ole Miss football fortunes plummeted after the glory years of 1954 to 1963, in large part because of the school's inability to attract top-flight African American athletes. The case of Marcus Dupree illustrates the point. Dupree was a very talented running back from Philadelphia, Mississippi, who was regularly compared to the All-American Herschel Walker at the University of Georgia. Schools from all over the nation recruited Dupree, including the University of Mississippi. However, when he developed a "short list" of 12 colleges, Ole Miss was not included. Mississippi State and the University of

Southern Mississippi (formerly Mississippi Southern College) made the cut, but not Ole Miss. Willie Morris followed Dupree's story. Having left the state in 1965, Morris returned to Mississippi in 1980 after having earned a national reputation as editor of *Harper's* Magazine and as an independent writer. He became writer-in-residence at Ole Miss, where he resumed his life-long love of Ole Miss football. In telling Dupree's story, Morris contended that 1962 and the images it conjured played a major role in Dupree's concerns about going there. Traditional symbols of the Old South remained, including the playing of "Dixie," the veneration of Colonel Rebel, and the proud display of the Confederate flag, all of which made one wonder about continued racial prejudice on the campus.[13]

Not only did Ole Miss undergo profound changes after 1962, so too did the State of Mississippi. One of the most significant effects of Meredith's desegregation of Ole Miss was that it triggered a public debate in Mississippi on segregation, white supremacy, and states' rights. Just as students disagreed over Meredith's presence on campus, all across the state people who had been silent in the past began to speak out. Since *Brown v. Board of Education*, the Citizens' Council and the Sovereignty Commission had been successful in stifling any opposition to their hard-line defense of what they deemed to be Mississippi's sacred "way of life." But, after the ugliness of September 30 at Ole Miss and the inability of Ross Barnett to either maintain law and order or stop Meredith from entering the university, reasonable people with moderate views began to express themselves openly. On October 1, the Monday after the Ole Miss riot, a group of 127 Mississippi businessmen met in Jackson in a moment of reflection on the state of events and for the purpose of resolving to pursue a new course. William Mounger, President of Lamar Life Insurance Company, spoke for many when in a television interview he said, "As a citizen of Mississippi, I apologize for not having spoken out. ... We adult leaders have failed our children. We have allowed them to be incited to the point where they themselves have caused violence and resisted the United States of America." When the group met, some wanted to censure Barnett, but in the end they stated their opposition to *Brown* while calling for obedience to the nation's laws.[14]

To be sure, extremists continued their attacks on all who voiced support of Meredith, integration, and the federal government, but theirs was no longer the only, or even dominant, voice. Moderates were speaking out. Like the business leaders in Jackson, most moderates were hardly rabid integrationists, but they were realists who believed that Mississippi was ill-served by continuing to fight the Civil War. They believed that integration was a new reality that could not be resisted, but they did ask for more time to prepare for further integration. All across the state, groups of moderates were willing to state their views publicly. John Faulkner, the writer's brother, agreed to an interview for the *Saturday Evening Post* after the riot. He said that for years he had been part of a group of Oxford citizens who met daily over coffee to discuss events. Every morning the group convened at Leslie's Drug Store, and as they departed each day they reminded each other that the Civil War was over, meaning that it was time to rejoin the union and embrace the future. After September 30, they voiced their belief that it was time for "responsible citizens" to stand up to the "riffraff" that they thought were responsible for the violence at Ole Miss. And they adopted a new parting slogan: "Lord, have mercy on us all."[15]

Black Mississippians were also more outspoken about educational opportunities in the state. To many, Meredith had given them more than hope; he had provided access. Dr. E. P. Burton, a surgeon in the predominantly black Delta town of Mound Bayou, discussed what school integration meant. "We aren't asking for integration for integration's sake," he said in an interview shortly after the Ole Miss riot, "but my son wants to be a doctor, so I send him to school in New York. Don't you think that if he could get a good education in Mississippi, I'd rather have him with me at home?"[16] Burton, like Cap Meredith, was a Mississippian who wanted his children to have the same educational opportunities afforded white children, no more, no less.

But Meredith's successful attempt to end segregation in Mississippi's schools also had unintended consequences. One of those was a political ploy by recalcitrant whites to convince the rest of the nation that the real issue at Ole Miss in 1962 had not been desegregation, but federal usurpation of state power, and that what happened in Mississippi could happen anywhere on any issue.

Just days after James Meredith entered Ole Miss, the Mississippi legislature passed House Concurrent Resolution no. 18 condemning the federal government's actions. Though a vote was not recorded, it is reasonable to assume that it was overwhelmingly in favor given that the membership had not changed since the same body gave Governor Barnett *carte blanche* in denying admission to Meredith. In the resolution, the lawmakers blamed the Kennedy Administration for violating Mississippi's state's rights and provoking the violence that occurred: "The law and order that prevailed at the University of Mississippi was rudely disturbed by the wanton invasion of the University campus by hundreds of armed federal marshals backed by thousands of armed troops, all under the direct orders of the President and Attorney General of the United States." According to "responsible eye-witness evidence," trigger-happy marshals started the violence when they "unnecessarily fire[d] tear gas shells into the backs of unarmed Mississippi Highway Patrolmen while said patrolmen were quietly moving said students away from the Lyceum Building." All of this was in service of an unqualified applicant. "This man Meredith," the legislators declared, "positively does not meet the qualifications of the University of Mississippi, applicable to all students." Further, "this man Meredith is in truth and in fact a ward of the President of the United States and his brother, the Attorney General, and he is, therefore, their direct responsibility." The resolution concluded by calling for the removal of Meredith from the university, the removal of federal marshals and armed troops from Ole Miss, and "reaffirmation" of the Tenth Amendment by Congress.

The desegregation of Ole Miss contributed to a new political discourse in Mississippi. Especially in making their case to a national audience, white Mississippi politicians interpreted events at Ole Miss almost exclusively on constitutional grounds, not in terms of race and segregation. What happened in 1962 was not about black and white, nor was it about an individual's claiming his civil rights; rather, they insisted, it was about the federal government's heavy-handed disregard for states' rights. During the crisis, Governor Barnett had not hesitated to use racist language to garner support for denying admission to Meredith. After he failed to maintain segregation at Ole Miss, Barnett continued to enjoy much support and admiration in the state, but his blatantly racist political style and rhetoric were soon jettisoned. Ross Barnett represented the old politics in Mississippi that the rest of the nation had long ridiculed, especially after watching the events of 1962 at Ole Miss. After leaving the governor's office in 1964, Barnett returned to his law practice in Jackson, where he resumed its leadership as the managing partner. But he also continued to speak out on behalf of states' rights and segregation. On one occasion shortly after he left office, he returned to Ole Miss, where he delivered a speech in Fulton Chapel. The auditorium had a capacity of a thousand or more, but on that occasion only a few score attended, including a row of black students and their friends. To the amazement of all attending, Barnett delivered the same speech that he had given hundreds of time before Meredith's admission. When he shouted the signature line: "Never, Never, will this great university be integrated," whites sat in stunned silence while the row of blacks stood and applauded in mock approval. Until his death in 1989, Barnett remained a popular speaker at political rallies across the state, where his voice was an echo of pre-1962 politics.

But, Mississippi politics had undergone a transformation after the integration of Ole Miss that was perhaps more apparent than real. That is, while there were new faces among Mississippi's congressional delegation, the younger voices sounded in many respects much like the older ones. Trent Lott illustrates the "new" politician who continued to exploit many of the same fears that older figures such as Senator James Eastland and Representative William Colmer had long voiced: fear of racial integration and fear of federal government intervention in state affairs. After graduating in 1963, the same year James Meredith graduated, Lott entered the University of Mississippi Law School, where he says that he became more conservative in his thinking. He said that the Law School had hired a group of "liberal" young professors from Yale who challenged traditional Mississippi understandings of the Constitution and civil rights. But, Lott contended, their instruction created a backlash in sentiment. "Instead of making us more liberal," he wrote in 2005, "they helped create a generation of thoughtful, issue-oriented conservatives who grew up to run Mississippi politics." After graduating, Lott soon found himself in the center of Mississippi politics in a career choice that would launch his long service first as a United States representative, then as a U.S. senator, and finally as Majority Leader of the U.S. Senate.

Though he would later characterize his move to the Republican Party as part of a widespread revolt against the liberal Democratic Party and its intrusive government policies, the evidence indicates that the ugly issue of race was at the center of the movement. Indeed, it would be his segregationist sentiments and ties that would lead to his fellow Republicans' ousting him as Majority Leader in 2002 for a speech he made with segregationist overtones. At a party celebrating Senator Strom Thurmond's 100th birthday, Lott recalled with pride that Mississippians had voted for Thurmond in 1948 when he ran as the segregationist candidate for the Dixiecrat Party and suggested that if other states had joined them, "we wouldn't have had all these problems over all these years." While Lott explained the comment as an innocent gaffe, he was soon at the center of a political firestorm when reporters discovered that he had made similar comments more than 20 years earlier while campaigning for Ronald Reagan in Mississippi. His memoir's comments on segregation notwithstanding, Lott had a long and consistent record on segregation during his days as representative and senator. In 1992, he was the keynote speaker at a meeting of the Council of Conservative Citizens, a successor organization to the Citizens' Council. He endorsed the group's platform as embodying the "right principles and the right philosophy." After his remarks at the Thurmond party, Republicans moved quickly to remove him from his leadership post because they had worked hard to portray the mass exodus of southern whites to the Republican Party as one based on principles of traditional family values, small government, and compassionate conservatism, not, as many charged, flight from the party that had fought for civil rights and voting rights for African Americans. To party leaders, Lott gave fuel to those who contended that race indeed colored the new Republican conservatism.

Beyond politics, Meredith's success at Ole Miss contributed to an important cultural shift in Mississippi, especially in the interpretation and writing of history. In 1962 Meredith wrote an important new chapter in Mississippi history by challenging largely unquestioned assumptions about race and authority, assumptions that many white ministers and politicians claimed transcended history itself. But after demonstrating that segregation's origins were indeed firmly rooted in history and could be ended through historical events, Meredith inspired African Americans to look afresh at the past as well as into the future. The result has been that blacks in communities all over the state have begun to challenge the "white" narrative by asking the most basic question: "Who gets to tell the story?"[17] As they retell the story,

African Americans not only challenge old interpretations, but introduce new actors in the state's past, recognizing the contributions of the labor, faith, creativity, and courage of those long ignored or ridiculed.

Whites have also begun to reinterpret history in light of the desegregation of Ole Miss. In a retrospective essay written for the twentieth anniversary of Meredith's admission, Bill Minor, longtime reporter for the New Orleans *Times Picayune*, assessed the changes inspired by the event. He called it a turning point in Mississippi history because it brought the state out of the shadow of the civil war and into the mainstream of America. So charged were emotions among white extremists in 1962, Minor recalled, that the riots came close to triggering another civil war. He characterized Barnett's defiance as leading an "emotional rebelliousness" similar to that a century earlier. For a time, a great many Mississippians dreamed of "winning" a war against the federal government, a dream that crumbled in "failure, riot, bloodshed and death." In the end, Meredith was admitted and graduated from the "pristine, all-white University. With his courageous act, Mississippi has changed greatly, most notably in the opportunities that are available to African-Americans." Yet, Minor cautioned, "Much of what has changed in Mississippi in the last 20 years, unfortunately, has come from mandates of the Congress or the federal courts. We have not done a great deal voluntarily on our own initiative." But, he concluded, Mississippi is no longer a closed society, he declared, "We have finally rolled back the Magnolia Curtain in Mississippi and opened the doors to the world." [18]

While the writing of history is changing, the currents of historical change in Mississippi are more resistant to change. For many white Mississippians, the integration of Ole Miss reinforced their commitment to states' rights and racial segregation. In 2001, Mississippians decided by a vote of 2 to 1 to keep the Confederate symbol on the state flag. By comparison, Georgians voted overwhelmingly to remove the symbol from their standard, again revealing Mississippi as a land apart even in the South.

As it did in Mississippi, the Battle for Ole Miss exerted short-term and long-term influence throughout the South. Its immediate impact was to stiffen the intransigence of arch-segregationists, some of whom had rushed to Mississippi to join the battle and, no doubt, returned home with new resolve to resist similar federal government encroachments. But James Meredith's admission to Ole Miss also provided inspiration for civil rights activists in neighboring states. Its symbolic impact can hardly be exaggerated. Even among southerners, Mississippi had long been regarded as a world apart, the staunchest and most violent defender of segregation. But events in 1962 meant that the South's seemingly impregnable stronghold of segregation had been breached. Those fighting for school desegregation in other southern states took heart; if the powers of Mississippi could be overcome, so too could those of other Deep South states. Despite the determined efforts of Mississippi's arch-segregationists as well as those from their allies from other southern states, Meredith had prevailed and Ole Miss was forced to admit black students. If it could happen in Mississippi, it could surely happen anywhere.

The Meredith case provided more than inspiration. It also gave rise to new weapons for fighting school desegregation in the South. Most importantly, it set federal courts in the South on a more aggressive course. Since 1955, southern federal judges had pursued the so-called *Brown II* doctrine of "all deliberate speed," thus granting southern school districts great latitude in avoiding or delaying desegregation. But, in ordering Governor Barnett and the State of Mississippi to enroll Meredith without delay, the U.S. Court of Appeals for the Fifth Circuit wrote a new chapter in federal–state confrontations. One interpretation of the Meredith case underscores its importance to the South: "In retrospect," wrote law professor Frank Read, "the trauma of Ole Miss seems to have stiffened the resolve of many federal judges to adopt harsh new measures to carry out their *Brown II* marching orders, and propelled the federal courts in the South to searching for new methods of implementation."[19]

While the Battle of Ole Miss had a profound impact on the campus as well as inspiring changes in the State of Mississippi and the South, it not only had a lasting influence on James Meredith—it defined him. That is, he will forever be remembered as the man at the center of the Battle of Ole Miss. After graduation, he moved on to many endeavors and careers, including that of lecturer, investment banker, restaurateur, radio and television repairman, farmer, entrepreneur (in businesses ranging from cosmetics to catfish), and founder of a religion (the Reunification Church Under God).[20] Some of Meredith's actions have mystified observers and invited criticism. He proclaimed himself a Republican, worked for a brief time for Senator Jesse Helms, and even supported the blatantly racist David Duke. Critics have offered various interpretations of what they regard as bizarre behavior; some see him as a mystic who claims to speak for the spirit of "his people," others see him as a publicity seeker who engages in strange behavior to gain attention for whatever cause he espouses at the moment, and still others regard him as mad. Meredith pays no attention to his critics. He remains as he was in 1962, a maverick who set his own agenda for his own reasons with little concern for what others might think. Regardless of what they think of his behavior after Ole Miss, civil rights activists recognize Meredith as one of the most courageous pioneers in school desegregation.

James Meredith's proudest moment at Ole Miss came not at the unveiling of his statue, but four years earlier when his son Joseph graduated with a Ph.D. in Business Administration. Not only did Joseph, a Harvard alumnus, graduate, he graduated as the Distinguished Graduate Student of 2001–2002. In an interview with *Jet* shortly after the occasion, Meredith said, "I was never proud of going to Ole Miss until my son graduated. I was humiliated." Forty years earlier he had waged war against white supremacy at Ole Miss. He now stated, "I think there is no better proof that white supremacy was wrong than not only to have my son graduate, but to graduate as the most outstanding graduate of the school." It was at that moment, he said, that he realized the magnitude of what he had done; the graduation of his son with full honors meant that he had won the battle, if not the war, for Ole Miss.

NOTES
....

Introduction
1. Cited in Neil McMillen, *Dark Journey: Black Mississippians in the Age of Jim Crow* (Urbana, IL, 1989), 232–233.

Chapter 1
1. The anecdote came from my interview with James Meredith, conducted on May 12, 2008, in Jackson, Mississippi.
2. James Meredith, *J. H. Is Born* (Jackson, MS, 1995), 7.
3. James Meredith, *Three Years in Mississippi* (Bloomington, IN, 1966), 19.
4. Chalmers Archer, Jr., *Growing Up Black in Rural Mississippi: Memories of a Family, Heritage of a Place* (New York, 1992), 69–70.
5. David Oshinsky, *"Worse Than Slavery": Parchman Farm and the Ordeal of Jim Crow Justice* (New York, 1996), 252.
6. Archer, Jr., *Growing Up Black in Rural Mississippi*, 17.
7. Anne Moody, *Coming of Age in Mississippi* (New York, 1968), 25.
8. Charles Evers and Andrew Szanton, *Have No Fear: The Charles Evers Story* (New York, 1997), 7.
9. Meredith, *Three Years in Mississippi*, 17–18.
10. See Martha Hodes, *White Women, Black Men: Illicit Sex in the 19th-Century South* (New Haven, 1997).
11. James Meredith, *Three Years in Mississippi*, 7.
12. Evers and Szanton, *Have No Fear*, 3–4.
13. Evers and Szanton, *Have No Fear*, 4.
14. Evers and Szanton, *Have No Fear*, 7.

15. Cited in Pierre Tristam, "By Any Means Necessary: Sen. Theodore G. Bilbo's Legacy of Hate," *Candide's Notebooks*, July 16, 2007.
16. Cited in McMillen, *Dark Journey*, 282.
17. *Greenwood Commonwealth*, June 30, 1899.
18. McMillen, *Dark Journey*, 72–73.
19. Archer, Jr., *Growing up Black in Rural Mississippi*, 111–112.
20. Archer, Jr., *Growing up Black in Rural Mississippi*, 117.
21. Evers and Szanton, *Have No Fear*, 38.
22. Meredith, *Three Years in Mississippi*, 15.
23. Archer, Jr., *Growing up Black in Rural Mississippi*, 117–118.
24. McMillen, *Dark Journey*, 113.

Chapter 2

1. James Cobb, *The Most Southern Place on Earth: The Mississippi Delta and the Roots of Regional Identity* (Oxford, 1994).
2. Willie Morris, *Good Old Boy: A Delta Boyhood* (New York, 1971), 14–16, 58.
3. Trent Lott, *Herding Cats: A Life In Politics* (New York, 2005), 7–9.
4. Lott, *Herding Cats*, 11.
5. J. Todd Moye, *Let the People Decide: Black Freedom and White Resistance Movements in Sunflower County, Mississippi, 1945–1985* (Chapel Hill, NC, 2004), 168.
6. Lott, *Herding Cats*, 14–16.
7. James Silver, *Mississippi: The Closed Society* (New York, 1964), 149.
8. Hodding Carter, *Their Words Were Bullets: The Southern Press in War, Reconstruction, and Peace* (Athens, 1969), 50.
9. Neil McMillen, *The Citizens' Council: Organized Resistance to the Second Reconstruction, 1954–64* (Urbana, IL, 1994), 175, 177, 179, 181.
10. Willie Morris, *North Toward Home* (Boston, 1967), 78.
11. Richard Rubin, *Confederacy of Silence: A True Tale of the New Old South* (New York, 2002), 96.
12. Morris, *North Toward Home*, 78–79.
13. Cited in Linton Weeks, "Mississippi's Senators Reflect Their State's Tradition and Division," *Washington Post*, January 7, 1999.
14. Trent Lott, *Herding Cats*, 24.
15. Willie Morris, *The Courting of Marcus Dupree* (New York, 1983), 241.
16. *Time*, November 28, 1960.

17. Charles Eagles, "The Closing of Mississippi Society: Will Campbell, The $64,000 Question," and Religious Emphasis Week at the University of Mississippi," *Journal of Southern History*, 67 (May 2001), 334.
18. Eagles, "Closing of Mississippi Society," 336–368.
19. Lott, *Herding Cats*, 23–24.
20. Morris, *North Toward Home*, 140.

Chapter 3
1. Evers and Szanton, *Have No Fear*, 60–61.
2. Evers and Szanton, *Have No Fear*, 62–63.
3. *Pittsburgh Courier*, January 31, 1942.
4. McMillen, *Dark Journey*, 262–263.
5. Evers and Szanton, *Have No Fear*, 55.
6. Evers and Szanton, *Have No Fear*, 57.
7. Evers and Szanton, *Have No Fear*, 64.
8. Charles Payne, *I've Got the Light of Freedom: The Organizing Tradition and the Mississippi Freedom Struggle* (Berkeley, 1995), 30–31.
9. Myrlie Evers-Williams and Manning Marable, eds., *The Autobiography of Medgar Evers: A Hero's Life and Legacy Revealed Through His Writings, Letters, and Speeches* (New York, 2005), 13.
10. Payne, *I've Got the Light*, 50–51.
11. Payne, *I've Got the Light*, 52–53.
12. Cited in Myrlie Evers-Williams and Manning Marable, eds., *The Autobiography of Medgar Evers: A Hero's Life and Legacy Revealed Through His Writings, Letters, and Speeches* (New York, 2005), 15.
13. Josephine Posey, *Against Great Odds: the History of Alcorn State University* (Jackson, MS, 1994), 31–33.
14. For King's sense of betrayal and outrage, see *Pittsburgh Courier*, March 16, 1957.
15. Evers-Williams and Marable, eds. *The Autobiography of Medgar Evers*, 204.
16. See Vernon S. Holmes Collection, Box 4 of 15, Mississippi State Sovereignty Commission, Special Collections, University of Mississippi Library.
17. For a discussion of the Little Rock case, see John Kirk, *Redefining the Color Line: Black Activism in Little Rock, Arkansas, 1940–1970* (Gainesville, FL, 2002).
18. Meredith, *Three Years in Mississippi*, 51.

Chapter 4

1. See Yasuhiro Katagiri, *The Mississippi State Sovereignty Commission: Civil Rights and States' Rights* (Jackson, MS, 2001), 55–61.
2. Cited in Bradley Bond, *Mississippi: A Documentary History* (Jackson: 2003), 239–240.
3. Katagiri, *The Mississippi State Sovereignty Commission*, 4–5.
4. Katagiri, *The Mississippi State Sovereignty Commission*, 5–6.
5. The Kennard case is covered in Katagiri, *The Mississippi State Sovereignty Commission*, 55–61.
6. Cited in James Loewen and Charles Sallis, eds., *Mississippi: Conflict & Change* (New York, 1974), 254.
7. Loewen and Sallis, eds., *Mississippi: Conflict & Change*, 256.
8. Silver, *Mississippi: The Closed Society*, 64–65.
9. Silver, *Mississippi: The Closed Society*, 66.
10. Silver, *Mississippi: The Closed Society*, 62–63.
11. McMillen, *The Citizens' Council*, 240.
12. McMillen, *The Citizens' Council*, 242–243.
13. McMillen, *The Citizens' Council*, 238–239.
14. McMillen, *The Citizens' Council*, 241.
15. Cited in Al Kuettner, *March to a Promised Land: The Civil Rights Files of a White Reporter, 1952–1968* (Montgomery, AL, 2006), 90.
16. McMillen, *The Citizens' Council*, 236.
17. See Michael Klarman, *From Jim Crow to Civil Rights: The Supreme Court and the Struggle for Racial Equality* (Oxford, 2004), 412.
18. "Strength Through Unity!" Address by Gov Ross Barnett to Citizens' Council Rally, New Orleans, March 7, 1960, Citizens' Council Collection, Folder 14, Special Collections, University of Mississippi Library.
19. See *An Introduction to the Knights of the Ku Klux Klan* in the Ku Klux Klan Collection, Box 1, Folder 1, Special Collections, University of Mississippi Library.
20. Meredith, *Three Years in Mississippi*, 4.
21. Loewen and Sallis, eds., *Mississippi: Conflict & Change*, 260–261.
22. Katagiri, *The Mississippi State Sovereignty Commission*, 106.

Chapter 5

1. William Doyle, *An American Insurrection: James Meredith and the Battle of Oxford, Mississippi, 1962* (New York, 2003), 52.

11. *New York Times*, October 21, 1962.
12. Cited in Barrett, *Integration at Ole Miss*, 71–72.
13. Cited in Barrett, *Integration at Ole Miss*, 72.
14. Cited in Nadine Cohodas, *The Band Played Dixie: Race and the Liberal Conscience at Ole Miss* (New York, 1997), 80–81, 86, 93.
15. Cohodas, *The Band Played Dixie*, 92–93.
16. Cohodas, *The Band Played Dixie*, 95–97.
17. See 1963 edition of the *Ole Miss*, the University of Mississippi yearbook.
18. *The Mississippian*, May 3, 1963.
19. *The Mississippian*, May 8, 1963.
20. Meredith, *Three Years in Mississippi*, 325–328.
21. David Sansing, *Making Haste Slowly: The Troubled History of Higher Education in Mississippi* (Jackson, MS, 1990), 195.

Chapter 8
1. Michelle Vance, "The 'New South' Begins with Monument Dedication," *The Daily Mississippian*, October 2, 2006.
2. I am indebted to James Meredith for providing me with a copy of the typewritten speech he had planned to give that day. It is entitled, "For The Dedication of the Civil Rights Monument at Ole Miss," 1 October 2006—James Meredith.
3. Evers-Williams and Marable, eds., *The Autobiography of Medgar Evers*, 293.
4. Cohodas, *The Band Played Dixie*, 107–110.
5. Townsend Davis, *Weary Feet, Rested Souls: A Guided History of the Civil Rights Movement* (New York, 1998), 217.
6. Cohodas, *The Band Played Dixie*, 134–135.
7. Cohodas, *The Band Played Dixie*, 123.
8. Cohodas, *The Band Played Dixie*, 122–125.
9. Meredith, *Three Years in Mississippi*, 19, 90.
10. Rubin, *Confederacy of Silence*, 42–43.
11. Cohodas, *The Band Played Dixie*, 128–129.
12. Evers and Szanton, *Have No Fear: The Charles Evers Story*, 128–132.
13. Morris, *The Courting of Marcus Dupree*, 294–295.
14. *Saturday Evening Post*, November 10, 1962.
15. *Saturday Evening Post*, November 10, 1962.
16. See Robert Massie, "What Next in Mississippi," *Saturday Evening Post*, November 10, 1962, 22.

17. See Emilye Crosby, *A Little Taste of Freedom: The Black Freedom Struggle in Claiborne County, Mississippi* (Chapel Hill, NC, 2005), 269.

18. Cited in "The Meredith Crisis in Retrospect: September 30, 1962—September 30, 1982," in *The Ole Miss Magazine*, September 30, 1982.

19. Betsy Levin and Willis Hawley, eds., *The Courts, Social Science, and School Desegregation* (New Brunswick, NJ, 1977), 16.

20. For discussion of Meredith after 1962, see Paul Hendrickson, *Sons of Mississippi: A Story of Race and Its Legacy* (New York, 2003), 167–172.

INDEX

....

Williams, Ben, football, 163
Williams, Chancellor J. D., urging
  courageous support, 106
Williams, Gransbill, prison gang
  labor system, 18–19
Wisdom, Judge John Minor
  Meredith's lawsuit against Ole
    Miss, 85–87
  overturning Mize's
    judgment, 96

World War II, blacks in military
  service, 51
Wright, Richard, *Black Boy*, 24

Y

Young Democrats, 161–163
Youth organizations, equal rights,
  92–93

22.95   11/19/09